WORK SUCKS!

A FUNNY VIEW OF A SERIOUS PROBLEM

SPENCER BORISOFF

Published by Richter Publishing LLC www.richterpublishing.com

Editors: Natalie Meyer & Monica San Nicolas

Cover Design: Mario Alberto Rodríguez Solano

Headshot Photos: Pierce Brunson Photography

ISBN:1945812427
ISBN-13:9781945812422

DISCLAIMER

This book is designed to provide information on the corporate work environment only. This information is provided and sold with the knowledge that the publisher and author do not offer any legal or medical advice. In the case of a need for any such expertise, consult with the appropriate professional. This book does not contain all information available on the subject. This book has not been created to be specific to any individual's or organization's situation or needs. Every effort has been made to make this book as accurate as possible. However, there may be typographical and/ or content errors. Therefore, this book should serve only as a general guide and not as the ultimate source of subject information. This book contains information that might be dated and is intended only to educate and entertain. The author and publisher shall have no liability or responsibility to any person or entity regarding any loss or damage incurred, or alleged to have incurred, directly or indirectly, by the information contained in this book. You hereby agree to be bound by this disclaimer or you may return this book within the guarantee time period for a full refund. In the interest of full disclosure, this book contains affiliate links that might pay the author or publisher a commission upon any purchase from the company. While the author and publisher take no responsibility for the business practices of these companies and or the performance of any product or service, the author or publisher has used the product or service and makes a recommendation in good faith based on that experience. All characters appearing in this work are fictitious. Any resemblance to real persons, living or dead, is purely coincidental. The opinions in this book are that of the author and not of the publisher.

"Oh, you hate your job? Why didn't you say so? There's a support group for that. It's called EVERYBODY, and they meet at the bar."

- Drew Carey

ACKNOWLEDGEMENTS

I would be an absolute moron if I did not start this section by thanking my fabulous wife, Helicia, for not buying into my entire family's claim that I am a very lucky man to have a woman of her caliber and she, well, not as lucky to have landed me. Despite the world that surrounds us generally agreeing with that exact sentiment, Helicia has always believed that there is something special buried very, very deep down inside me and for that, along with infinite other reasons, I am both deeply in love with her and eternally grateful for her. This book could never have happened without all of the sacrifices she has made. I also have to tip my cap to her for having the patience of an inanimate object as evidenced by our 31 years together. Thank you, babe, for being my very best friend, a great mother, and the most beautiful human being inside and out.

This book is the brainchild of a conversation that took place nearly a decade ago between me and another best friend, Paul Weiner, after I discovered Paul reading a book that was written by a college classmate of mine. Disturbed that this old University of Pittsburgh classmate was on his third best-selling novel and believing that I was a better writer than him, Paul convinced me that I should prove it and write a book where my expertise lies: hating work. I pitched a first chapter to Paul and was off and running. Thank you Paul for being tapped into this project from day one and all throughout and believing that I have a voice that the world simply has to hear.

I also have to thank my father for being the one family member that believes that Helicia is lucky, too. He has always set a great example for me as an independent thinker with the guts to stand by unpopular opinions. Thank you, dad, for listening to my chapters over the phone, sharing your feedback and believing that I am on to something special here.

Last but not least, I would like to thank Tara Richter and her publishing team at Richter Publishing for all of their hard work and expertise on bringing my book to market.

DEDICATION

This book is dedicated to the millions of people who contemplate sucking on an exhaust pipe when their feet hit the floor on Monday mornings but keep going into work each week because they have families to provide for. God bless you all!

CONTENTS

FOREWORD

Written by my father, Grammy nominated musician Len Barry.

Sweat was dripping slowly under the doctor's fogging glasses. The droplets continued, crawling both under and over his tightly tied white mask. His nurse, much less responsible and into this miracle, stood dry as a bone at the patient's feet. She was pushing the visitor's legs apart at the knees.

The patient lay tense and terrified on the table crying, cursing, and sweating – really sweating. I, having been invited to watch and in no pain at all, was cool, calm, and mildly empathetic. Actually, I was thinking that even though I grew up with and was married to the lady lying on the table, it was the first time I'd ever seen her without makeup, false eyelashes, and a hundred dollar hairdo.

"Not long now," the doctor mumbled.

"Push, push," the unconcerned nurse cajoled.

"I *am* pushing, God damn you!" screamed my wife, Elaine, the lady on the table.

It was June 2, 1969, and soon my son, Spencer, would pop out and pop into our lives. Little did the infant, who was about to experience his "coming out" party, know what he was "coming out" into. He was about to become the son of a father who lived to hear himself on the radio and a mother who loved to look at herself in the mirror. I, his father, was a semi-famous recording star, and Elaine, his mother, was a diva – a self-appointed diva. Hey, we were nice people who were, at that time, not ready to sacrifice for little Spencer and his slightly older sister, Bia. We were the opposite of doting. Let's say, we were the anti-dote.

Spencer grew up mostly thanks to his grandmother's love and his own intellectual curiosity. He always was cocking his head and looking at a normal situation, silently wondering: *How did you all come to that decision?*

He would educate his rebelliousness at Kobe's Lower Merion High School and then at The University of Pittsburgh, where he studied journalism. Eventually, he married his college sweetheart, Helicia, and fathered his daughter, Baye. He is the best husband and father I've ever seen: attentive, giving, loving, and caring. He is everything I never was. I guess I was his "what not to be like" role model.

Spencer still looks at the world with that cocked head and the prevailing question: *Hey, what's going on here!?* I can't help looking back at that June 2nd scene in the OR and picturing his reaction to being slapped on the butt by his doctor, catalytically evoking his first breath and words could he have spoken.

"Hey, doc," he would have bellowed, "you didn't have to do it that way. You could have just done it this way," he would have directed, cocking his head.

PREFACE

Ahhh, the sounds of hammers hammering and electric drills spinning from my dad's workbench as he polished off another pleasurable play project for my sister and me.

Oh, the sound of mom humming happily as she fluttered around the kitchen taking little tastes from big pots of another of her delicious dishes.

I should still be able to hear the ignition crank and purring motor of the family station wagon at 7 a.m. as Dad headed off to work. Mom's voice should still echo in my mind's memory saying, "Hi, hon, how was your day?" when Dad returned after a long, hard productive stint. These are the sounds of childhood, the auditory scrapbook of a young boy's role models paving the way. What great memories, you say? I agree. Except the only hammer I heard in my house was M.C. Hammer singing "Can't Touch This." You see, my father didn't fix things, he created things. My mother never ever fluttered around the kitchen in her life, except to put T.V. dinners in the freezer for her kids to heat up. The family station wagon, which was a secondhand Oldsmobile, didn't take nobody nowhere at 7 a.m., and certainly not to work, because 7 a.m. in my house was like 3 a.m., with hours of z's left.

Dad didn't deal with alarm clocks. He never needed his dreams jolted by its insulting clangs at some ungodly hour to wake him to go to work. My father didn't have to go to work because he didn't have a job. He was unique, unprogrammable, and original. He had a vision that took x-rays of people and situations, not pictures. He was a writer and poet, a producer of magical pages of mesmerizing tunes and tales that were once just empty vacuums of yellow legal pads. He was a dreamer who made records, hit records, gold records from puffs of smoke that most never saw.

My dad was so creative, people sometimes underestimated his intellect and opted to classify him as just plain nuts. But Dad didn't care what other people thought of him. In fact, fitting into the mainstream –

whether socially, intellectually, or morally – was something he flat out refused to do. He did not believe in adherence to predefined structure. He could not follow someone else's path. He was an independent explorer. His mind went places most people never thought to go. When he shared his outrageous ideas, most people laughed and dismissed him as kidding. He wasn't kidding. He thought of the airplane not as a great invention, but as the great destroyer of man's quest to fly – by himself – encased only by God's heavens. His unconventional outlooks were extreme, but the truth is, he was a history and political science buff, an encyclopedia of lands, leaders, and early life on this planet.

His heroes were Abraham Lincoln, John F. Kennedy, Leon Trotsky, Sun Yat-sen, Willie Mays, and Wonder Woman. He predicted that labor unions would price American automakers out of business. He called Communism's collapse while lauding some of Karl Marx's progressive visions. He intellectualized that labor-based society, not religion, was the opiate of the people. He delineated its absurdities and marveled at man's adherence to it. He, however, would have none of it.

Unfortunately, I was not so lucky. While my father was dreaming his way through life, I was preparing for it. I graduated college with a bachelor's degree in journalism, which readied me to be a newspaper reporter straight out of school. Unfortunately, the curriculum failed to teach me how to live on the breadcrumbs that cub reporters writing for weekly suburban publications were paid at the time. After four years at the news desk, a taste for cushy living led me away from writing toward sales in corporate America where a man could get P-A-I-D. What followed was more than 25 years of gut-wrenching nausea, infinite disgust, and constant frustration; an endless string of days of absolute dread caused by the unfathomable formula that makes up big business. It was unbearable. It was everything my father had said he hated.

I asked my dad once how he knew corporate America was so awful, since he'd never worked a normal day in his life. He explained it with sincere, insightful, recall.

"Son," he said, "when I was a boy, every time I wanted to play with my father, I couldn't find him. When I asked Nan where Pop was, there was only one answer: he was always at work. I know my father loved me," my dad romanticized, "I saw the proof. His timecard. He worked his life to the bone and my life to lonely. My dad was kind, witty, and sang like a bird, but I never had the joy of laughing with him or doing duets. He was used and ultimately used up by a system some pseudo intellectual aristocrat devised to keep his spoiled ass in ruffled grandeur. Well, son," my father finalized, "after growing up as a mamma's boy with my dad M.I.A., I swore I would never let work do that to me."

So, you see, I had to write a book that would expose the insanity of our work-based existence while causing readers to evaluate the need for a more reasonable labor system. It's my DNA, my predetermined perspective further embedded by two and a half decades of experience in the corporate world.

I am my father's son. I have a young heart and a free mind. I'm free to disagree. I look at the worlds "tote that barge and lift that bail" and wonder why the man can't tote his own barge. I look at alarm clocks and time cards and bosses and see them as rude, insolent insults to man's dignity.

I look out at tomorrow's horizon and sometimes I'm afraid, not because my book won't change the world, but because the world isn't going to change me. What will I do, you ask me? Well, I'll tell you. I guess I'll just spread my wings and fly. That'll be me outside your Delta window flying by on my way up!

~

I won't wear orange. It is a nice color for a summer sunrise, but it makes a lousy jumpsuit. Nor will I wear stripes with stripes, especially if the outfit has a long number stitched across the chest. I don't like eating from tin trays on long tables that are bolted to the floor. Even less is my desire to sit on a lidless metal toilet while being watched by a tattooed homicidal roommate who thinks I am taking too long. There are nearly 3,000 inmates on death row in the United States – I should not be one of them. I have killed no one. I have broken no laws and have committed no crimes. Still, I have done my share of hard time.

At 22, I graduated college with my bachelor's degree and shortly thereafter was apprehended by the corporate world. I went quietly at the time because it is not in my nature to cause trouble. Although chained to a desk for more than eight hours a day, I decided not to fight the system. I kept my head down and followed orders, like the others, for several years before finally realizing that I could be a lifer. I may never be released. So, I escaped, promising myself I would never go back inside. My mind and body were liberated: fresh air, long naps, free choice to do as I pleased. I was at large and in charge – until I turned myself in. I felt guilty for violating culture's code, so I went back to the working world, intending to be a model prisoner. But the system broke my morale. I worked around the clock under precise instruction to perform ungratifying tasks at a high level to serve the interest of the institution. Five days out of the week for 50 weeks out of the year, my interests were irrelevant. So . . . I paroled myself. Needing money, I went back. I hated it. Different prison, same schedule. Breaking rocks all day with little thanks. An ignorant warden with lots of rules. In by 8. Out by 6. An hour for lunch. Meetings. Performance Reviews. Reports. Rush hour. Alarm clocks. The Sunday night shakes. I couldn't be more unhappy. I broke out again. Then I returned to corporate America, kicking and screaming. The pattern repeated over and over again for 25 years. Nearly 30 different jobs, never fired. I found jobs because I am capable and charismatic, but left also because I am capable and charismatic. No matter how many times I was sentenced to a life of hard labor, I knew deep down inside that I didn't do anything wrong, that I didn't deserve to be punished like this, and that I, like all of us, deserve better. My body may have returned to work time and time again, but my mind was never imprisoned. Being committed to a life dominated by involuntary labor is no way for free men to live.

There are millions of Americans out there serving heavy time in our corporate system who are torn up by their life sentences. I know because I've been locked up with many of them and I've heard them mumbling about the violation of their human rights in the deep dark corners of their solitary confinements. I call on you now, my innocent friends, to take off your orange jumpsuits and get in line. Stand there in your underwear and, when it's your turn, give the system back its uniform.

Turn around and take a deep breath of freedom.

Many men have died for it.

It's time for us to live for it!

"Kill my boss? Do I dare live out the American dream?"

- Homer Simpson

What I wrote . . .

Form Letter

Letter of Resignation
(Only the names and dates change)

10/11/17

Maude Norton
District Sales Manager
Waste Removal Systems, Inc.
301 Park Blvd.
Pinellas Park, FL 33765

Maude,

I regret to inform you that I have decided to resign from my position as Territory Sales Manager with Waste Removal Systems, Inc.

As a professional courtesy, I am offering a two-week notice to help transition my work in any manner you see fit, with the understanding that the company will pay me my October commissions, expenses, unused vacation/sick time, as well as my final paycheck for my last two weeks, upon my departure.

It has been a pleasure working for the company over the past four years. I have grown both professionally and personally while employed with the organization which means I have invested my time wisely with no regrets.

In my opinion, you have been an excellent manager who has made my time with the company a fair, informative, and respectable work experience.

I wish you success in all endeavors you undertake. It has been an honor working both with you and for you and I hope to keep in contact in the future.

Thanks again for the opportunity to work at Waste Removal Systems, Inc.

I will remember my years here fondly,

Spencer Borisoff

What I felt . . .

Letter of Resignation

Actual Translation

10/11/17

Maude Norton
Incompetent Manager
Waste Removal Systems, Inc.
301 Landfill Lane
Cesspool, FL 58426

Maude,

It is with tremendous relief and an unfathomable amount of pleasure that I giddily inform you that I have decided to resign from my enslavement as an order taker with Waste Removal Systems, Inc. This is actually the happiest day of my life by leaps and bounds, far ahead of both of my other favorite days: the day I got married and the day my daughter was born.

Because I want two additional weeks' pay for doing absolutely nothing at all, I am offering a two-week notice so I can tell my next employer that I handled myself professionally upon resignation and left the company on good terms. It is my honest hope that you will reject my notice and instead ask me to immediately leave the premises while still agreeing to pay me my October commissions, expenses, unused vacation/sick time, as well as my final paycheck for my last two weeks that I never had to work.

It has been a total nightmare while being held captive by the company over the past four years. I have grown in no way, shape, or form – neither professionally nor personally – while employed with the organization, which means I have grossly wasted my time with every possible regret.

In my opinion, you have been a useless manager who has made my time with the company an unimaginably demeaning, degrading, and disgusting work experience.

I wish you complete failure in all endeavors you undertake. It has been a joke working both with you and for you and as a result, I hope never to see you, hear from you, or think about you ever again. The thought of this place will always sicken me.

I sincerely wish we never would have met,

Spencer Borisoff

"When you go for a job interview, a good thing to ask is if they ever press charges."

- Jack Handy

THE JOB INTERVIEW

Relationships built on lies are never a good thing. In matters of love, such relationships often end in divorce; if not, double murder-suicide. Where work is concerned they invariably end badly as well.

This is a disaster, I think to myself while smiling enthusiastically at my interrogator as he lays the ground rules for what seems like a terribly laborious procedure. Today's interview is with a Fortune 100 payroll processing firm that has been voted one of the Top 50 best companies to work for. I can't help but think if the interview process is this much of a pain in the ass, then actually working for the company could very well be the true manifestation of my ultimate nightmare. I wonder how many roofies the voters of the Top 50 survey were slipped before having pens stuck in their hands.

The lies actually begin before introductions are even made. I walk into the shiny glass office building wearing an expensive two-buttoned black pinstriped Theory suit that I picked up from Neiman Marcus along with my crisp white dress shirt, a Brooks Brothers grey silk tie, and a perfectly polished pair of Perry Ellis dress shoes. Carrying a black leather briefcase and a phony but convincing air of confidence that says if Cochran, Shapiro, and Bailey had not gotten O.J. off then I certainly could have, I extend my right hand.

"Spencer Borisoff here for an 11:00 interview with. . . with," I momentarily stutter as my surprised eyes register the extent of her magnificent beauty.

Completely aware of what had just happened, the receptionist interrupts through a sexy subtle smirk revealing cotton white teeth that are even straighter than the flat-ironed, caramel-colored hair framing the face of an angel.

"Mr. Hassel will be with you in just a moment," she assures with denim blue eyes peering out from razor sharp bangs that nip her dark, jungle-lush eyebrows. "We're glad to have you," she finishes while gently waving her tan, taut arm like a Showcase Showgirl toward a lobby seat.

And all this could be mine if . . . Mr. Hassel shows more promise than his name, I laugh to myself as I prepare to sling my first verbal lie.

"Glad to be here," I say. The words that passed through my lips could not be further from the truth.

Truth is, I would rather be sitting on a scorching Florida beach during the Ides of August wearing my fully zipped down ski coat, wool mask, insulated mittens, and ski boots locked into my skis than be here today. This place is everything I am not. It is a mass of metrosexual money mongers mixed with finely built fashionistas who play strictly by the rules of corporate culture while selling their souls by dangling their curves to close deals. As employees pass by me while awaiting my looming tussle with the third degree, it becomes apparent to me that working here would be like working with a bunch of Terminators coated in fragrant flesh of varying degrees resembling David and Victoria Beckham. Ah, so beautiful on the outside but so evil on the inside, programmed to stop at nothing to make big bucks for the company and a little coin for themselves. Corporate robots. For now. One day they will all self-destruct and be left as sheared shards of flesh and bone and metal to be swept up by the janitorial crew.

Damn, even with a mop and a bucket he looks handsome, I think, as the maintenance man rolls on by.

Chameleon-like, I blend in beautifully today. But the warped mind inside my blond, blue-eyed, exercised 6-foot frame believes that this would be an exhausting way to live. I strongly consider walking out, but it's too late. I am called back to the conference room and here I am, staring at a man who is aptly named by the kindest standards. To me, the word "hassle" implies a minor inconvenience, but I am quickly under the impression that this guy could be a major problem.

"Sounds great, Mr. Hassel," I say in response to the litany of steps that need to be taken to go through the interview process. I know right then and there that I will not be working for this corporation. *Admittance into the FBI Academy is probably no more stringent,* I think while digesting the seemingly endless list of evaluation protocols: two in-person interviews (one with anal Jonathan Hassel and a second with his boss, the district vice president), a drive-along day with an outside sales representative, a math test, a personality test, a drug test, a work history and criminal background check, reference checks, and a PowerPoint presentation by me on why I am the best candidate for the job. It strikes me as funny that the one component of the screening process that should unequivocally be utilized, they don't have – a polygraph test. Tisk-Tisk. I can easily lie my way through the interviews and trudge my way past all the test and checks, but even then, a job offer is quickly rewarded with a two-week intensive classroom training and testing course in upstate New York. I am more of a downtown Vegas kind of guy. Gotta draw the line somewhere, and there is no way I'm leaving my wife and little girl for two weeks to study subject matter that would entice me to stick a loaded revolver in my mouth.

"All right then, we'll start by going over your work experience," Hassel says in a stern but soft voice, brown eyes bulging a bit with focus. His red power tie is pulled up so tightly against his Adam's apple that I wonder if he can breathe. *God, what I'd give to see this guy pass out and bang his head on the edge of the conference table,* I silently muse. If he cuts his skin, I am confident I will see signs of a machine under there.

He continues, "Then I will ask you a series of situational questions that will give us a good idea of how you have handled specific business scenarios in the past."

If this guy were a plant, he would be a cactus because he is one dry prick. I think I would rather work as a transvestite for a pimp named Nasty than work for this handsome henchman.

"Let's do it," I say pleasantly while momentarily fantasizing about sexing up that delicious receptionist.

For starters, Hassel inquires as to why I left my previous job. I contemplate sharing the truth, but opt against it. Telling him that I'm not the kind of guy who takes crap and that I'd eventually quit when I found out that a GPS tracking application was surreptitiously activated on my company-issued cell phone, catching me going to the gym one day and catching up on my sleep the next – during work hours – certainly won't be received kindly. So, I do what all job candidates do best. I lie. I consider fabricating that my former employer hesitantly asked me to leave because my sales numbers were so much higher than everyone else's that I was consequently destroying office morale. Instead, I tell the hiring manager that I left because there were no opportunities for future growth; that financially, I had been earning at the top of the pay scale because our commissions were capped; and as a top producer, I am confident that I can make a better living and greater contributions to a highly respected firm such as his. That, I figure, sounds a lot better than the truth that if I stayed one more day at my company I very well may have broken every bone in the general manager's face for invading my privacy by activating surveillance software that tracked my every move. I put up with the abundant meetings and unrealistic quotas, the relentless reports and insulting performance reviews for four years, but their Orwellian big brother power play was a mustard gas red line that I couldn't allow them to cross. The other reps felt similarly, but didn't have the guts to stand up for themselves for fear they would lose a job they all hated anyway. A sad bunch, really. Truth is, I was a top producer for my last company. I did exceed quota on a regular basis and I made a decent living there. But an outside sales representative should be judged on production rather than location, so I decided not to buy the gas mask and wait to see if my skin would begin to blister before my lungs exploded.

Not the kind of story that gets a job seeker fast-tracked to an offer. I have no doubt I made a good decision not to go there with Hassel, for he would certainly have little patience for nonconformity. A few minutes later, I realize I am making a horrible mistake while completely exposed to a rapid-fire barrage of questions that revolve around my past accomplishments and future goals. If I just told the man the truth, I could have been halfway home by now. I don't want the job, anyway. *They do everything but scan your retinas here,* I say to myself, as the lies keep coming.

"Describe the perfect job for you," the mannequin-like manager instructs.

I would like to tell him the truth, that that job would be one that lists the term "lying down" in its description and that I am having an awfully difficult time finding it on LinkedIn and Ladders. Instead, I tell him that it is an opportunity where I can apply my lifelong sales experience in my new role while continuing to learn from those around me as I help the company grow exponentially.

I tell lie after lie after lie after lie. I say that I enjoy cold calling, that I usually make 50 or more sales calls a day, that I believe sales meetings are great because we all get to share ideas that can help each other out, and that I am an early riser and that being in the office by 8 a.m. every morning is perfect for me.

Now, before you judge me too harshly, let's not forget that Hassel, on behalf and with the full endorsement of his Fortune 100, Top 50 Places to Work company, is doing the exact same thing – lying his ass off. He tells me that if he hit the lottery, he would still choose to come here to work every day. I wonder if he is mentally retarded for thinking I would ever believe that lie. His sales reps, he says, like to wear a suit and tie to work every day when what he really means is that nobody complains out loud about the mandatory business attire dress code. Another twisted lie. He says his team members can't wait to get into the office to start their days each morning and that they don't mind coming in on Saturdays if they need to catch up on some work. I am pretty sure that his tight tie is cutting off oxygen to his brain. He seems demented as he explains that morale is high and turnover is low. If that's the case, I wonder why I have seen this same job posted month after month for the past two years on all the internet job boards known to mankind, from Tenney, Minnesota (U.S. Population: 5) to the Middle Eastern province of Qatar.

An invisible layer of clarity clings to my clean-cut, angular face as we agree to meet for a second time next week with his boss. My last lie for the day and the last one he will ever hear from me in person. But it won't be the last lie that Jonathan Hassel will ever hear or tell because another candidate will be coming to visit with his briefcase of bullshit sometime soon. And maybe, just maybe, after all the tests and checks and interviews and applications, that candidate will be hired. Then, it will be just a matter of time before the boss and his subordinate see a familiar look in one another's eyes as they pass each other in the hallways: *Not quite what I expected*, their eyes will silently shout. *Not exactly how we covered it in the interview.*

Fewer people would hate their jobs if companies and candidates would stop lying to one another during the interview process, I think as I walk out into the lobby.

My big blues lock on the receptionist like an F-16 Fighting Falcon locking missiles on a Russian MiG.

"We'll see you soon," the sexy cyborg says.

The thought gives me goose bumps, but I can't help but tell the truth. It's been two hours.

"No you won't, Angel," I say, and rush home to lie down.

WORK SUCKS!

What I wrote . . .

Form Letter

Post Job Interview Thank You Letter
(Only the names and dates change)

12/05/17

Jonathan Hassel
Division Sales Manager
Payroll Pluss+, Inc.
15906 Corporex Plaza.
Tampa, FL 36710

Jonathan,

It was a pleasure meeting with you on December 4th to discuss potential employment with Payroll Pluss+, Inc. as a territory sales manager for the Tampa division.

After interviewing with you, I am certain that the territory sales position would be a tremendous career opportunity for an extremely motivated, highly credentialed and seriously dedicated business professional like myself. I am impressed by the accomplishments, the environment, and the people at Payroll Pluss+, Inc.

It is only after careful consideration, however, that I have decided to accept an offer from another highly regarded firm at this time. I hope to keep the door open for future possibilities between us.

Thank you for taking the time out of your busy schedule to meet with me, and most of all, thanks for the opportunity to interview at Payroll Pluss+, Inc.

Best Wishes,

Spencer Borisoff

What I felt . . .

Post Job Interview Thank You Letter

Actual Translation

12/05/17

Jonathan Hassel
Grossly Uptight Manager
Payroll Pluss+, Inc.
15906 Corporex Plaza
Thunderstorm, FL 36710

Jonathan,

It was a total hassle meeting with you on December 4th to discuss modern-day enslavement with Payroll Pluss+, Inc. as an everyday beggar for the division where it torrentially rains at 4 p.m. for five months straight each year.

After lying to you and with you for nearly two consecutive hours, I am certain of nothing other than knowing I would rather take my chances wrestling rabid crocodiles for a living than work with you and your Maybelline crew. I am turned off by the accomplishments, the environment, and most of the people at Payroll Pluss+, Inc., except for the receptionist out front who I nicknamed "Angel" and haven't stopped thinking about for even one second since sprinting out of your building.

It is with absolutely no thought whatsoever, but with Puma-like instincts, that I have decided to sit on my couch and gorge myself with trans-fat laden comfort foods for the next 30 days in an attempt to recover from the post-traumatic stress symptoms I have suffered since being exposed to the possibility of living life as a robot at your firm. There is no other offer from even a shady outfit, let alone a highly regarded corporation at this time. I hope I have made it clear that the door to future possibilities between us can be considered boarded up, chained and padlocked, with no key in the universe capable of sliding in its keyhole.

I sincerely wish we never would have met,

Spencer Borisoff

P.S. That extra "s" on the end of the company name is asinine and bothers me to no end.

"Cursed is the man who has found some other man's work and cannot lose it."

- Mark Twain

DAYBREAK

I am not a bird. I do not spend my nights nuzzling in a nest in some tree high above. Nor have I ever spread wings and gracefully flown in formation with the rest of the flock. But mostly – despite all my confusion as to what I am – I know that I am not a bird because I do not sing song as an announcement to another sunrise. No, daybreak usually finds me bed-stuck, focusing on the ceiling, daring it to fall down on me as an alternate form of agony. The wooden ceiling fan, powered high, could be swapped out for one with blades of machetes and I would not change my mind. Like a defiant prisoner of war bravely guarding a nation's secrets, I merely grit my teeth with a steely stare and challenge my punisher to bring it on. I am not scared because I endure worse pain on a regular basis. Much worse. Both the ceiling and its rotating confidante know there is no use. Their brand of physical torture cannot compare to the deep internal wounds I suffer at the hands of a guilty conscience from voluntarily leaving job after job and breaking the heart of a wife who continues to stand by me. As an act of spite, not mercy, the beams above back off and allow me to rise.

My stomach sinks as I head to the sink. New week, same old story: going to a job I hate as much as the last one, same as I will the next one. I know my days on this security system sales job are numbered because feigning interest in the corporate cause is shredding my sanity as if my mind were a sunbaked block of cheese rubbing up and down a brand new, industrial-sized grater. *How do other employees live this lie without either breaking down or hating themselves?* I ask myself while spitting my toothpaste out with extra oomph in protest of all of the pretenders in the workplace. Funny thing is, no matter how hard I seem to brush or how many times I spit, I can't seem to get the terrible taste out of my mouth that a weekday morning invariably brings. Desperate to extinguish the foul flavor, I grab the plastic bottle of Listerine that has been sitting in my medicine cabinet since the Clinton presidency – because I can never quite bring myself to use it – and take a swig, careful not to swallow even the slightest bit of the poison. My mouth instantly begins to sizzle and burn as if I had gulped gasoline and Pop Rocks all at once. The pain becomes more severe with every swish. Tears fill my eyes in a matter of seconds and my legs begin to wobble. I think I feel my gums receding and my teeth loosening and I wonder if one hour of continuous gargling would erode me to the point that I would look like the Crypt Keeper from that spooky 1990s HBO television series *Tales from the Crypt*. Maybe so, but I'll gladly take my chances and rinse with it all day long as a substitute for having to go to a job I hate. In fact, if some kind soul would offer to pay me, I would guzzle the mouthwash for a living instead of being some flunky in corporate America. For some reason, the pain of swallowing a petro-chemical seems easier to endure than living a life that revolves around someone else's agenda. Case in point: It is 7:26 a.m. and my cell phone is making more noises than the Benny Goodman Orchestra did in its heyday. It's ringing, clanging, buzzing, beeping and chiming, chock-full of emails, text messages, voicemails, and meeting invitations. I am interested in none of it and consider flushing my work-issued iPhone down the toilet with my morning pee.

I ignore the impulse and instead reach for the shaving cream, foam up my face and grab a razor, tempted to drag its edge horizontally across my jugular in retaliation against the Molotov cocktail of emotions threatening to blow my world sky-high. I am fighting an uncivil civil war against myself, constantly wavering between two evil choices: do I sacrifice my own happiness in exchange for providing comfort and security to those I love, or do I wave my own flag and charge ahead, believing that if I keep going, I will eventually win a better way of life for me and my family? I do not know the answer to that, but I do know that I am in a constant state of suffering from my struggle, battle-weary from firing blanks at my own feelings which have proven to be a most worthy enemy. I am embarrassed that I am not more successful. I am ashamed that my wife is the rock of the family instead of me. I am disappointed that I have never found my niche in the working world. I am bitter that so many others hate what they do and just accept it as a necessary evil, as I believe there is no honor in surrender. I am disgusted that others judge my constant search for a better alternative as weakness instead of strength. I am proud that I am a free thinker with a mind of my own. I am anxious, not knowing what the future will bring. But mostly, I am tired of smelling the world's morning breath when I open my eyes at sunrise. I have more than enough Listerine, and I am extremely willing to share.

I hop into the shower and scrub away yesterday's filth to make room for today's. I towel off, throw on some slacks and button up an oxford tight to my throat. I loop a tie around my neck and can't help but see the similarity between heading off to work and going to the gallows pole. Either way, I find it near impossible to breathe with sympathy in short supply. I pull my laces tight as if trying to strangle my shoes so they will be unable to carry me to my dreadful destination. My soles are unfazed and quietly lead me to the front door, being careful not to wake my little one. There is no time for breakfast because I milked all of my minutes by begging my bedroom walls to collapse all over me. Truth is, I don't have the stomach for a morning meal, anyway.

My chest is already smothered in heartburn and with more on the way, compliments of morning traffic, there is certainly no need to add grease to the blaze. I reach for the door knob and shake my head, asking why I put myself through this terrible torture.

"Daddy, Daddy, wait!" her little voice screams, "I want to give you a kiss before you go."

I bend down and steal a smooch from my baby girl before walking out the door with my answer.

WORK SUCKS!

"Why do they call it rush hour when nothing moves?"

- Robin Williams

RUSH HOUR

So many hearses and not enough early morning road. It's not that the thousands of death vehicles clogging the streets are stretched too long for all to fit – because these hearses are not stretched at all. Nor do they have heavily padded raised leather roofs, curtained back windows, or flapping flags formally announcing a somber parade in honor of the recently deceased. No, these hearses blocking the boulevards are not a part of one gigantic memorial procession. Each vehicle, instead, is separately transporting a body to a grave. Strangely, none of the bodies are cold, stiff, or deadly still. Nor are they resting comfortably inside quilted caskets in the back of long funeral carriages, because these bodies are breathing, very much alive, voluntarily driving their cars, trucks, SUVs, and minivans to their own burial grounds. But they are not en route to cemeteries or their final resting places. And as miserable as most of the drivers are, they are each thankful to be burying only a tiny piece of themselves today, just like yesterday – and like tomorrow. It is rush hour and everyone is headed to work, slowly dying by spending another dismal day on the job that they can never get back to live the way they want to live it.

Their anguished faces say it all. Odd, but even though I make this drive every morning, I haven't noticed this much self-induced mass pain since I channel surfed and accidently landed on the shores of The New York City Marathon on ESPN 19 last year. *I've never seen a smiling jogger*, I think to myself as I witness a blinkerless idiot manage to block two lanes of traffic to a dead stop while attempting to maneuver his white, convertible hearse to a left lane that seems to be momentarily moving one-half of a mile-per-hour faster than the lane he so desperately wants to desert. The irony strikes me square on the jaw as I let the imbecile merge in front of me because I am in no hurry to get into an accident or into work. Everyone else, however, seems to be in a horrible, hostile hurry. This, in my opinion, is because when faced first thing every morning with the prospect of enduring another day of work whoopings, people tend to be instinctively tentative to leave their homes and go take their beatings like a man. After a last second dismissal of the temptation to stay home by mustering every ounce of human resolve in their bodies required to walk out of their doors, everyone is invariably running late, which leads to a chronic case of morning rush hour traffic. Ironically, this leaves the country's workers crammed on crowded roadways, trying desperately to get to places they don't want to be. Having to tolerate rush hour to get to work is akin to enduring basic training before being dropped into an enemy jungle. One horror is worse than the next. Only a mannequin could remain in an unaffected mood facing these circumstances, and being that none of us are stationed in the windows of downtown department stores, it is easy to see that having to endure this daily routine before even arriving at the office critically poisons the possibility of job enjoyment. To make matters worse (yes, it gets worse), those who manage to make it to work early are rewarded with an even longer work day than the sadistic lunatics in charge even imagined, while those who arrive late risk being interrogated like some prisoner of war by deranged lieutenants in the corporate chain of command whose unwavering allegiance to the company borders on insanity. Getting to work on time is a game of Russian roulette, *Deer Hunter* style, and I can see the desperation on each chauffeur's face as they drive themselves to another day of dying.

Much to my chagrin, traffic starts to break up a bit and my meat wagon begins to move at a quickened pace. Normally, I can count on one hand the number of cars that pass me while I'm driving. On my way home from work, the only vehicles that go by me have sirens and flashing lights on their roofs. No one is in more of a hurry than me to see their wife and kid at the end of the day. I'm on the clock and I don't want my life to tick away from me, so I put my pedal to the metal in an effort to maximize my personal time. Heck, even when I have nothing particularly important to do or nowhere to go, I drive fast. The one exception to the rule is when I drive to work. Almost everyone passes me on my commute to the office. Senior citizens pass me, nuns pass me, and even some bicyclists pedal past me. I drive slowly simply because I hope never to arrive. Reverse is the preferable direction to travel when the alternative is driving forward toward work. Fortunately for the multitude of companies I've worked for, I happen to be a very punctual guy and am rarely late. But in those few instances that I am tardy, I do not panic at the thought of repercussion. The "boss," as an authority figure, means absolutely nothing to me. Truth is, I fear punishment from my manager less than I fear a lollipop from a bank teller. Replace him or her and the next boss will just be another manager I ignore. The standard corporate policy of tying workers to a clock is merely a common bullying tactic that consistently eats away at office morale as sure as a team of termites will swallow a home's wood frame.

In my eyes, the harshest penalty for corporate disobedience – termination – is more like a temporary gift than a punishment because of the tremendous relief one can feel knowing that a recurring bad dream is over, even though there are no guarantees that they won't experience similar occupational nightmares in the future. Further, I find it ironic that management likes to flex its muscle by threatening to permanently remove people from a building that they constantly attempt to sneak out of anyway (smoke breaks, early lunch, "doctor's appointments," etc.).

It is upsetting to know that millions of American workers are trapped in a reality where they live in fear of losing a job that makes them feel as hollow as a drinking straw in an empty glass. The thought of most

American workers never finding their professional niche is a difficult drink for any compassionate human being to swallow. But the higher ups at many American corporations are eager to take a swig from that warm bottle. Company chiefs have figured out a formula that enables them to fill their bellies while keeping their employees thirsty – and that is how our American corporations and the chief executives who run them get rich. Corporations pay their employees just enough money to get by so they have no choice but to come back to work for the rest of their lives and help build the company's wealth. And the majority of the population has settled into this scheme nice and not-so-cozy because as cruel as the system is, it is much easier to fall in line than to step out and demand change. After all, no one wants to be living under a bridge or – even worse – found hanging from one some morning.

My entire body aches and I can't help but think it is because I have been digging my own ditch daily for longer than I wish to remember. Work has managed to siphon the life out of me, but I know I am not alone. I stop at a red light (I actually do follow some rules) and notice a middle-aged woman in the death-mobile next to me brushing foundation across her pale face like an embalming artist applying makeup to a corpse for final goodbyes. I want to say a prayer for her and for everyone else gradually decomposing all around me. But instead, I just mind my business and pull up to my own plot on a familiar, grim graveyard.

I am at work.

WORK SUCKS!

"An alarm clock is a device that makes you rise and whine."

- Anonymous

ALARM CLOCKS

Being awoken by the reveille of an alarm clock at the hint of daybreak to go to work is vile and sickening and would be only moderately tolerable if the siren were set to get me to a scheduled orgy with Heidi Klum, Gisele Bündchen, Adriana Lima, and the rest of the Victoria's Secret All-Star lingerie modeling crew.

I think we can all agree that being *forced* to go somewhere, whether at gunpoint or due to a more benign necessity, diminishes the appeal of that destination. That is precisely the case with daily work coercion. An abrasive buzzer or even a hand-picked musical tone, set to jolt us out of unconsciousness, is the first injustice of the work day as well as a seed of drastic dissention that is so prevalent in the workplace. The dreaded wakeup call is an initial indication that *having* to go to work is about as appealing as going to the electric chair, if not less so because of the absence of a decadent last meal like lobster, filet mignon, and a banana split sundae. Oatmeal and toast at sunrise just doesn't appease a dead man walking quite like surf and turf. Nor can the condemned be convinced to accept a callous fate with merely a muffin and a half of grapefruit.

There are very few pleasures in life that rival sleep. Arguably, a phenomenal meal can be equally gratifying. Indisputably, great sex or even not so great sex – let's just say any unforced sex – surpasses sleep on the delight meter. It's a stretch, but I will concede that perhaps a couple of other life luxuries register on the same Richter scale as sleep, but undoubtedly hitting the hay and staying in the hay until getting up voluntarily is an elite pleasure. Undoubtedly, this is one reason that the prospect of enjoying a job is doomed from the very, very beginning. Simplified, work directly interferes with sleep – an extreme pleasure – and as a result, we hold a lifelong grudge against it.

Alarm clock sabotage is a vicious killer of innate enthusiasm and high spirits. Men who climb mountains voluntarily cannot climb out of bed in the morning when they must because they must. Now, I'm not saying that I climb mountains, but I have indeed spent a lifetime climbing out of bed in the morning prematurely. As a result, I would like to share with you my state of mind as I proceed through a typical work day. I concede that my feelings tend to teeter on the extreme end of the spectrum, but my instincts tell me that living a life dominated by involuntary labor is taking an enormous emotional toll on tens of millions of Americans who can directly relate to my bloodbath of a daily struggle.

My phone alarm sounds and after tapping the snooze button anywhere from one to three times to delay my inevitable torture, I rise with a raw, unfiltered bitterness for reasons covered above. I proceed to my window, peer out at my driveway, and pray that my Acura is gone, stolen overnight. I have insurance and would gladly spend the day at home on hold for hours with Nationwide, impatiently waiting to listen to their nonsense in order to register a claim rather than go to work.

Unfortunately, that never happens, so I make the drive to the office hoping to pass a garbage bag bursting with a dead body on the side of the road. I'd be pleased to deal with the onslaught of police questioning and nosy news crews that come with this fiasco in lieu of even spending a Friday at the office, let alone a Monday.

Of course, that also never occurs, so I proceed to the office and wish for the building to be on fire upon arrival. The customary temptation to call for help or douse the flames with the outside hose would not even cross my mind. Instead, euphoria even thicker than the billowing black smoke would smother my smiling face as I watch the building burn down to a pile of glowing embers.

Since this gift is not bestowed upon me either, I then go inside, put my briefcase down and contemplate conspiring with a fat, sweaty customer service representative (who hates work as much as I do) to fake having a heart attack directly outside the boss's office in an effort to cause enough commotion to warrant an early release for the day. (Note: if an early dismissal were to be granted, this would only be because the company is concerned about the legal ramifications of the incident and its overall reputation, not the physical and emotional well-being of its employees.) *Maybe if I capture his act on video with my cell phone, the footage could go viral on YouTube and he could shoot to social media stardom and hire me as his manager*, I chuckle to myself, while picturing him up on an awards stage making an acceptance speech, dripping wet like a defrosting meatball.

Day after day for more than two decades at many different jobs, I am plagued by this line of thinking in a sad effort to will myself out of work. Maybe a hurricane will hit. Perhaps an uncle will die; he lived a long life. On the positive side, when you live in the suburbs, you tend not to go to many funerals in the first half of your life, but, on the downside, nor can you capitalize on an excellent excuse to take a solid three days off from work.

In case I haven't made myself clear yet, I believe that corporate careers, broken down to their uncooked core, are merely a form of institutional imprisonment. It is because of rules, regulations, policies, procedures, supervisors, reports, goals, performance reviews, meetings, more meetings, and even more meetings, that – on days when I must be in the office – I crave my lunch hour like it's a conjugal visit with my sandwich. There is a little foreplay, spreading the mayonnaise and licking the dripping edges in anticipation of this reward for good behavior. I indulge quickly and completely, being left with a deep sadness eclipsed only by a deeper need to rush to the bathroom. I then return to a 6x6 foot cubicle and fight off the unending urge to sleep until my five o'clock parole is granted along with the other corporate inmates. One condition must be met, however. Be back bright and early and do it all again. No exceptions. No excuses.

For now, I will be back. My family needs to be fed. My little girl needs to be clothed. A mortgage needs to be paid. So, due to an inherent survival instinct, both I and the American worker will do what needs to be done. Amend that. We will do the minimum that needs to be done, not because we are unskilled or lazy but, mostly because we are angry about *having* to go to a place called work that if given our druthers would otherwise be buried on our things-to-do-list.

Now I'm not saying that I'm not a warm and caring individual, because I am; just ask my wife or daughter. However, for two plus decades, the morning buzzer has instantly turned me uncharacteristically cold and careless by ordering me to rise with the roosters. That sadistic siren not only breeds contempt for a job regardless of the nature of the work to be done, but also explains why product quality is down, morale is low, service is sloppy, and mistakes are the norm and not the exception in the American workplace.

Simply stated, I do not want to be bugled out of bed in the morning unless my job entails oiling up supermodels for a swimsuit shoot. (By the way, if anyone is hiring, please contact me IMMEDIATELY! I can always write on the side.) I assure you that finding a job as a lather man is a very difficult task, which explains why I have destroyed more alarm clocks than I care to count since graduating college 27 years ago.

WORK SUCKS!

I'll Get up for Love

She climbs into bed beside me
And kisses me on my cheek
"Get up, get up" she urges
I act like I'm still asleep

She mounts me like a pony
And rides my eyes awake
Daylight starts dancing
The bed begins to shake

"Sleepy head" she giggles
Ticklin' me as she rides
She laughs, whines and wiggles
I open up my eyes

I look up at love
She looks down at me
That's how I get up
On weekends when I'm free

I don't need no buzzin'
Or ringin' in my ears
"I love you – I love you daddy"
Is all I need to hear

Reveille's for soldiers
Alarm clocks are for fools
They're both a bad beginning
To days that are just plain cruel

My lady and my baby
Are my responsibility
The life my family lives

Is largely up to me

So take away the trumpets
And disconnect the clock
The ringing' and the buzzin'
Have simply got to stop

You took away my freedom
To feed your greed machine
But don't mess with my self-respect
Or interrupt my dreams

Don't ring – don't buzz
I'll get up – I'll get up
I'll get up for love

"A meeting is an event where minutes are taken and hours wasted."

- James T. Kirk

MEANINGLESS MEETINGS

No one croaked, nothing burned down, and my car was not hot-wired, nor did my bedroom ceiling fall down upon me. So, here I am, with morning crust still wedged in an eyelash or two at first assembly of the day in a sales meeting. This Wednesday morning gathering begins like all the other forgettable roundups, with a whole lot of fat chicks sitting around a rectangular cherry cedar wood conference table, eying a big box of Dunkin' Donuts that they are too embarrassed to dig into. As they harness their temptation to devour the dough by looking away as if being needled for blood, I can't help but wonder why they practice this pointless pantomime. We all know they are big-boned. Not medical condition big-boned, overeating big-boned. Certainly they are not dieting. They are no lighter than they were last week; or any week, for that matter. If they are dieting this ineffectively, *that's* what's embarrassing. Furthermore, it always amazes me that when donuts are sitting out in plain view in a room full of people, no one is interested in eating them. But, if you put them out in the break room after the meeting is over where people can nab one somewhat secretly, they seem to disappear in less than a minute. *They're just donuts, people. Really, it's no big deal. Someone please take a damn donut already so my head will stop hurting.*

My thoughts are thankfully distracted, but unfortunately it is by another phenomenon that I do not understand: office laughter. This is an oxymoron and absolutely makes no sense to me at any level. There is nothing funny about being somewhere you don't want to be. A dental patient does not laugh during a root canal, a claustrophobe doesn't laugh before being slid into a closed MRI machine, and I don't laugh at work. Let's get one thing straight. I am a real funny guy. I find humor in most anything, have a genuine talent for making others laugh, and am the type of person that can lighten the mood using humor in virtually any situation. People like having me around because of my innate sense of humor. Yet, where work is concerned, I am not a "ha-ha" guy. The premise that I must devout 10 hours a day to serving a company or else my family doesn't eat is not amusing, but dead serious. I do not find work funny and I do not find work fun. Jokes that make me laugh on the weekends do not even move my lips during the workday. Let me elaborate. If the late great standup comic George Carlin were onstage at The Improv and I was lucky enough to be in attendance, I would likely spend that hour bent over in my chair half falling onto the floor holding in my pee from uncontrollable, hysterical laughter. Now, if the same comedian, George Carlin, was in the lobby of my work performing the same routine on a Monday morning, at no point would I even crack a smile. I am not kidding you. Why? Because there is absolutely nothing funny about the venue. A courtroom convicted criminal does not laugh when he is being shackled away to serve his time. Jerry Seinfeld could be in the jury box swapping barbs with Cosmo Kramer and it would not change a thing because death row just doesn't get a lot of laughs. Never has. Similarly, work is a lifetime sentence and not a laughing matter. It's hard to laugh when I feel like vomiting all over everything and everyone around me.

My feelings are not all that bizarre. Case in point: If every person in the office were given the choice to either stay for the day and continue to work or leave for the day with no consequences, I guarantee you that in 30 seconds flat the only thing left in the building would be that box of donuts (which still no one in my meeting has touched). It is an absolute fact that no one wants to be here. Office etiquette dictates, however, that forced smiles and fake laughs are encouraged corporate behaviors. This conduct drives me insane because I am the type of guy that does not bother faking it. In fact, it takes all the constraint I can muster not to headbutt an employee when they laugh at work. (Now that may be something I would laugh about at work.)

My name is called. My head hurts even more now as I realize the meeting has been in full stride for quite some time and I haven't even noticed due to my self-induced haze. It's okay though, because I travel down this sunless street regularly and I know how to cover my ass. It's actually pretty easy, because almost no one is listening. As my clouds begin to part, a welcomed thick fog rolls in on the rest of the group. It's like this every week.

I start to talk and the rest of my coworkers begin to fade away into their own little perfect storms. For five minutes, I talk about my pipeline, my recent sales, future revenue forecasting, and some lost deals. The information I spew can be easily reviewed in salesforce.com, an internet-based customer relationship management (CRM) database that my company pays big dollars for so sales reps can keep track of their prospects and the company can keep track of their sales reps. A less dysfunctional and more competent upper management team would realize that a huge benefit of the robust capacity of salesforce.com is to eliminate time consuming sales meetings just like this one. But that would mean the end of free donuts. So, instead, I am under a microscope that is way out of focus, but no one seems to have the energy or desire to adjust the knob that will make the image I am presenting more clear. I make my activity seem more hearty than it really is, just like everyone else, and give my boss a few nice nuggets that she will in turn exaggerate, embellish, and aggrandize when she attends her next meeting to report to her superiors. That is what these types of meetings are all about. They are merely a way for middle managers to prove to upper management that they are actively managing their people. Period. Nothing more. This meeting is not helping anyone's productivity, sharpening skills, or moving the proverbial ball forward – indeed, nothing of worth is getting accomplished. On that note, I think it's also important to bring to light that nobody in here cares about the company's vision or the company's bottom line. We only care about our own bottom lines, which ironically, are in direct opposition to the interest of the company. Corporations exist to make money, not spend it. Our salaries are an operating expense, which means that satisfying our interests means sacrificing their own. In Corporate America, that doesn't happen. This is another primary example of why the average corporate employee can never get ahead and why the relationship between Corporate America and the standard American worker is doomed from the very beginning.

This crazy game of charades continues as my boss goes through the motions too, asking me a few cursory questions about the competition's pricing and my proximity to quota that I am prepared to answer by using corporate-speak that sounds meaningful but in reality is totally devoid of substance. I tell her that other suppliers are offering the same service for a little cheaper but I am able to get around that by selling our superior customer service and asking prospects probing questions that give me the angles I need to make powerful presentations and close deals. She likes that and tells me I'm doing a nice job. She asks the rest of the group if they agree with my insightful approach (even though I have presented absolutely NOTHING of substance). They nod like beaten up boxers curled up in their corners when asked if they are okay to go out for another round. They barely know where they are, let alone the details of what I said. None of that matters, though. All I know is that I am off the hook again until this Friday when we all have to go through this meaningless exercise again – only this time, with more intense daydreaming by the gallery with the weekend on the horizon. We all made it through another useless meeting that won't change or improve a thing.

My boss ends the needless suffering on a positive note. She tells us it was a good meeting and jokes that it seems like we are all working too hard. A colleague laughs. I think real hard about stuffing a chocolate covered cream donut in her mouth to shut her up (I know she wants one anyway), dumping the remaining donuts on top of her head and bonking the flimsy box into the side her face. This mental image would usually bring a smile to my face, but alas, I am at work, thus not here, not now. I remember I have a family to feed, clench my teeth, and walk out of the conference room door, dreading my upcoming pointless performance review scheduled in half an hour.

"I pay no attention whatever to anybody's praise or blame. I simply follow my own feelings."

- Wolfgang Amadeus Mozart

PERFORMANCE REVIEWS

If I wanted to be *judged*, I would have learned to walk in heels, thrown on a killer dress, and entered a transvestite beauty pageant.

If I wanted to be *scored*, I would have carefully waxed my groin along with the rest of my body, wiggled into a slick Speedo solar brief, and joined the Olympic swim team.

If I wanted to be *rated*, I would have chosen X-rated and taken off my clothes for the camera while jumping in bed with the adult film industry.

But I don't want to be critiqued. Never did, which would explain the missing pumps, goggles, and towel, as well as the absence of a cheesy moustache between my nose and upper lip. What doesn't make sense, however, is why I am sitting three feet from and directly in front of a panel of one that is concentrating, at the moment, on assessing my "core behaviors" over the past year.

"To what extent would you say that you provide a clear and consistent message in the work environment?" my boss asks while leaning forward on her flabby forearms like some sort of oversized rocking horse.

I pause for a moment before answering, awaiting elaboration, because I genuinely have no idea what she is talking about. When clarity isn't offered, I opt not to translate her tongue like some kind of naval seaman interpreting Morse code, but improvise instead.

"Well, Chief, as you know, I've never wavered there, on that point since the day I joined the organization," I say, looking directly into the prescription lenses that are clamped down on the bridge of her wide nose, "I've said from the get-go that this whole shindig here, work, is just a bit unbalanced in favor of the company. Now, have we done anything about lengthening lunch hour and shortening the work day since I brought it up at this time last year?" I ask, while leaning back in my chair and raising my left eyebrow a la *Star Trek*'s Mr. Spock, making light of what is, to me, an absurd exercise.

She tries to keep a straight face but cracks a smile, not because of my oddball perspective, but rather because she enjoys making her employees squirm over the prospect of paltry raises that, once taxed, will be barely enough money to pay for a couple of used tires.

"Maybe we should add a 'sense of humor' criterion to bolster your score," she says, insinuating that my already minimal pay hike is about to be a penny shy of enough coin to get a gumball.

"Well, I know how much you like to laugh," I respond, truly believing that upper management gathers each morning in a back room somewhere to laugh uncontrollably at the returning laborers as they file in like zombies to be victimized yet again by corporate exploitation without so much as an audible whimper. They laugh so hard that they can barely get their words out: "They're . . . back . . . again," the brass wail, gasping for air while holding their sides from the pain of continuous laughter. "They . . . actually . . . keep . . . coming . . . back," they convulse, abdominals in full contraction, marveling that such a sinister system has subsisted without resistance for so long.

I tell my manager that she should write the sense of humor category into the performance review right now and get it over with, sarcastically citing my instincts to take swift and definitive action when the need arises.

"Between my production and my humor skills, I should be making as much as you next year," I say, continuing a verbal joust that has been in full swing for about an hour now.

I have made it Windex-clear that the premise of analyzing a human being, in an effort to fine-tune his performance like he is some sort of Italian sports car, is a repulsive idea in and of itself. I mean, the company should be tickled pink that anyone with a heartbeat and a pulse is willing to continually offer their services – at any level – while getting such a raw deal. But the concept of being examined by a severely flawed individual who has the power to judge me without the capability to improve me triggers an immediate gag and vomit-burp reflex just behind my Adam's apple. Truth is, I don't want to be "improved" to meet some silly work standard anyway. I sell enough product to hit company sales goals and I amuse people, without intending to, with my bizarre notions. That is what I do. I have never been interested in the rest of the rules.

"Your production certainly isn't the issue here," she says, in a corrective tone that escapes from her wrinkled throat, "it is your attitude. Your negativity about work policy and procedures filters down to the rest of the team and endangers the integrity of the environment," she scolds, while red-marking my evaluation sheet for further emphasis.

It is ridiculous to me that my boss actually thinks that I am the reason that everyone in our department is so damn dour at work. The others are more than capable of figuring out that working around the clock for relatively meager wages while taking orders, being talked down to, and continually dissected is pretty much a bum gig. When an employee who gets only two weeks of vacation a year is denied a requested day off because someone else on the team is already going to be out of the office that day, it becomes spotlight-bright that the rules are rancid. They don't need me to tell them what they already know. It's not that they are unaware of the lunacy of it all, it's just that they've made a choice, as have I. We all need the money, so we put up with this nonsense, this insanity called work. We've made a decision to come back again and again because we need to eat and like to sleep in a warm bed, preferably not alone. So, we've reached the conclusion that it's better to swab the decks than it is to walk the plank. Certainly, that is no secret. It's just that if you hand a guy a mop and tell him to produce a shine, the least that you can allow him to do is complain a little – and that's where I come in.

Decision or not, quantum physics is less difficult for me than getting out of bed at dawn to go to work – and I am completely incapable of processing complicated science. In fact, if management even had the slightest idea of the severe emotional and psychological pain I overcome daily in order to commit myself to the workday, then they would immediately cancel all my performance reviews and just stand and applaud me as I enter the building each morning. If they truly figured me out at my deepest and most intimate level, if they could climb inside my body and actually feel the heroic effort it takes to continually bring myself to the office, then they would know that the greatest accomplishment they have ever witnessed in the workplace is my arrival each morning and would commemorate my achievement by erecting a bronze statue in my likeness to be planted on the dead grass just outside the front entrance. But these people, these managers, are in such a fog that they are hard to impress. Nothing new. Heck, even the captain of the *Titanic* overlooked the iceberg at first.

It becomes painfully obvious that my statue isn't coming when my boss tells me that I could be more detail-oriented and further explains that I need to put in "extra effort" when required. I know quite well that I have no "extra effort" to give, that I use it all up refraining from quitting on the spot, slashing the boss's tires, and turning over every desk in this place, leaving me utterly exhausted. As a matter of fact, I'm exhausted right now, so much that I'm willing to forego my miniscule raise if I can just get the heck out of here. I have four new tires anyway.

"I'll work on that," I say insincerely. "Are we through here yet?"

"Just one more thing before I let you go," she says, while capping her red pen. "This year I expect action, action, action!" she yells like some sort of crude pornographic movie director demanding an unnecessary do-over.

"I'll give it to you just how you like it," I tell her, wondering why it has taken me so long to start growing the moustache.

"Life spent in constant labor is a life wasted."

- George Jean Nathan

THE SYSTEM

Befuddled, I often wonder how this preposterous arrangement of five days on and two days off came to be. I picture a corrupt and powerful dictator, revered by the people, on the verge of addressing the masses. He arises from a deep night's slumber with the remnants of the world's finest hand-rolled cigar perched precariously atop an African mahogany nightstand to his right and a devastatingly fine female laying dutifully naked to his left. Scared to dress before it's okay, she watches the ruthless ruler, her husband, slide off their seamless silk sheets and into his satin slippers, violet velvet robe with matching crown, and approach the balcony doors. Tens of thousands below begin chanting his name as they catch a glimpse of his shadow bending up his bedroom wall and onto its cathedral ceiling. He stops in his tracks, and then begins nodding his head in unison with the crowd's cadence. He looks back toward the bed, not at his wife, but at the six-foot long, gold-framed life-sized painting of himself hanging above the canopy.

"I am their master," he says, "whatever I tell them, they will do. I am their king and they will love me."

He looks at his beautiful wife demanding approval and she sheepishly smiles on cue. He turns toward the French doors and she winces at the thought of what is coming: an extraordinary crime against humanity. The public, three stories below, grows louder as they see his royal image through the glass doors. He swings his bedroom doors open and walks onto the sun-splashed balcony with both arms raised in the air, acknowledging his fearful followers. He holds a platinum staff in his left hand and puts his right index finger to his rotten red lips. The crowd goes instantly silent. He speaks.

"We will be the leader of the modern world. We will lead by example. From now on, our citizens will work harder than the rest of the world, longer than the rest of the world, with fewer breaks than the rest of the world."

The mob goes insane with approval, knowing that any opposition will most surely bring immediate death.

The dictator continues. "There are 52 weeks in a year and the great people of this great nation will work 50 of those weeks. There are seven days in a week and the great people of this great country will work five of those days. There are many hours in a day and the great people of this great land will work from sunup to sundown. Our nation will prosper; your life will have everlasting meaning."

The masses jump up and down, hugging one another with great emotion – as if they have just been told that each of them has been bequeathed a fortune in gold – making sure their leader can see. And their ruler is pleased. Pleased with the fraudulent financial arrangements he made with his country's crooked corporations and pleased that his petrified people would never disobey him for fear of the ultimate consequence.

And so it is, the origin of the 50-week work year, the five-day work week, and the all-day work day. Agree to work 96% of the weeks of the year or else be executed, an easy choice considering the alternative. Now it all makes sense to me.

Or perhaps there is another explanation for the insane demands of our work-based existence. Perhaps, in an effort to avoid nagging side effects, every politician, secretary, lobbyist, campaign volunteer, security guard, and parking lot attendant on Capitol Hill went off their medications at the very same time, leaving our political hub without a sane mind capable of interjecting any sense into anyone at all. A whole bunch of depressed, paranoid, obsessive-compulsive, schizophrenic, panic-stricken politicians then proceeded to pass The Fair Labor Standards Act (which ironically is very unfair) that dictates our outrageously consuming standard work schedule. But the good news is that none of our elected officials had dry mouth while speaking in favor of this ludicrous arrangement. Personally, I'd rather walk dizzily around profusely sweating, with diarrhea, acne, a constant urge to pee, and every other medication side effect in the book than work five days out of seven days for 50 weeks out of a 52 week year. This is nuts! We live in America. Our leaders don't wear robes or crowns in public or kill defiant citizens on command. A handful of our officials probably have gaudy self-portraits hanging in their halls, I'll give you that, but at least they're not in the pockets of our great corporations. Ooops. Where was I? Oh yeah, the heads of our government do not give orders to shoot down pissed off people in the streets. So where, when, and at what time is the anti-work rally? I'll bring the mimosas. *"Anyone . . . anyone . . . Bueller . . . anyone?"*

Just what I thought. There is no rally planned, is there? I know, it is darn near impossible to partake in an organized protest against work when you have to be at work, so instead of defiantly demonstrating in our streets and demanding a more equitable system for ourselves, we will just keep on softly complaining about our overbearing work schedules until we either have heart attacks or reach retirement, whichever comes first. Some of us will die and the others will wish they had, because I have a news flash for you: *This just in,* (for the first time since the last time it was just in a few moments ago) *most Americans **HATE** their jobs.* Every business environment that I have ever worked in – and I have worked in many – has been saturated with employees whispering for the weekend and counting down the minutes to 5 o'clock. American workers do everything but yell "Yabba-Dabba-Doo" and slide down purple dinosaurs at quitting time. Heck, employees would get into stone and wood cars and foot pedal themselves Flintstones-style out of their work parking lots to get home if they had to.

Perhaps this is the price we pay for being the economic leader of the free world. Our leaders obsess over being the premiere global power on the planet. Me, I just want a few extra days off – each week. Think about it rationally for a second. A fair deal is usually a 50/50 split. An equitable arrangement set up between work time and free time should mirror this percentage. Simply put, there are seven days in a week so the American worker should be expected to work three and a half days. There are 52 weeks in a year, so maybe we could devise a plan where our citizens work only 26 of those weeks. Now, I'm just spit balling here. There are countless ways that our crooked system could be straightened out; made to be more fair and better balanced. I know this might seem like a gargantuan concession for our government to make on behalf of its people, but that is only because we are so way off-base to begin with. I think it's doable. All the government has to do is realign its priorities a little so that the people's happiness is equally important as our greedy ambition to rule the world.

The papers I hear shuffling in the background are undoubtedly the nation's tax records of every citizen of our country. The screaming I hear are the voices of our leaders shouting that more time off for our workers translates into less production and fewer tax dollars collected which would in turn create a financial disaster for our country. But I'm here to tell you that fewer hours worked and more days off doesn't have to mean less tax dollars in the nation's coffers. No, refreshed workers are invigorated workers capable of out-producing tired, bored drones that are just going through the motions because they have to. Passion brews production and people who are focused and want to work because their lives are fairly balanced will generate more revenue than uninspired, lazy laborers that work nonstop.

I believe our great country can fiddle with the fractions and still remain a powerful global presence. Other economies endure worldwide despite fewer demands on workers. In France, for instance, the standard work week as dictated by French Employment Code is 35 hours. In the United States, a 40 hour work week is standard for the typical American worker, and we all know that many of us work even more, uncompensated. By conservative calculations, the extra five hours a week that American corporate employees work translates into an additional 31 days of work annually for Americans. That's a whole month's worth of extra work for us each year. How did that happen? On top of that, French law guarantees full-time workers a minimum of five weeks' vacation per year, while many of their companies extend up to eight weeks of vacation in addition to a dozen public holidays. Now that translates into as much as four times more vacation time for the working French than we offer working Americans. Additionally, French workers who log more than 35 hours a week are entitled to added time off. Still, with all this time off, the French economy is the second largest in the Eurozone after Germany. German workers also work an average of 35 hours per week, with an average of 24 paid vacation days. According to the International Labor Organization, Americans work on average nine weeks more per year than Western Europeans. Now, I've never been a big proponent of France, and even less so of Germany. Much less so. No, I'm an American, born and bred. But just because I'm an American doesn't mean I can't admire and applaud the way another country treats its people. I believe that deep down, American citizens don't care about being the big bully on the block, they just want more time off work to enjoy their families, their hobbies, and the only lives they have to live.

We elect our public officials in this country. Politicians should need to meet the people's demands in order to stay in office. Our next president could run on the platform of changing the work week from five days to four days and win the popular vote by a landslide, no matter what his stance on abortion, healthcare, global warming, fossil fuels, or foreign affairs. Book it. If he changed the work week to three days, his children and their children would also become presidents one day.

Until that day comes, however, Americans are going to keep working virtually around the clock day after day, week after week, and year after year.

No, they don't gun us down with a firing squad in broad daylight here. They prefer a subtle torture and a slow death.

I'll take the cigarette and blindfold, please.

WORK SUCKS!

"All work and no play makes Jack a dull boy."

- Jack Torrance, *The Shining*

THE SUNDAY NIGHT SHAKES

The depression is severe, and sometimes, on rare instances, it comes bundled with a cold sweat that leaves my body shivering and the sheets soaking wet. But tonight, I am not panicking at the hopelessness of it all. Tonight is just a typical late Sunday night that has me lying in a dry bed, wide-awake, staring at the ceiling, wondering where the weekend went and how I can get it back. *I would cross the barren desert of Giza*, I tell myself, *in search of a long lost genie lamp that could help me extend my abruptly withering weekend.* Upon discovery, I would frantically rub the bottle and mumble through sand-scratched teeth, *"Wish one: let the weekend start over."*

In fear of jeopardizing consent by asking for too much, I would then quickly revise my first wish and ask for only one more day off, *"just one more day,"* I would pathetically plead. That seems like a reasonable request, certainly worthy of being granted by a long-abandoned genie trapped at the bottom of an ancient brass bottle. Of course, all along, while rubbing, I would silently be wishing for my genie to pop out in the exact likeness of a 1960's Barbara Eden, star of that old sitcom *I Dream of Jeannie*, arousing outfit and all. I wonder if part of a genie's arsenal of powers is an ability to read minds and if so, I hope she won't consider my secret craving for a stunning appearance as an official wish and count it against me. I can use all the wishes I can get, so I wouldn't want to waste one on such a petty preference. And who's kidding who here, anyway? With my luck, my wish granter is more likely to resemble Rosie O'Donnell, in a genie bikini top and all. I shudder at the thought, but more so at the fact that no genie is going to save me from having to go back to work once again, bright and early tomorrow morning.

I refocus my thoughts as my eyes look through my sliding glass bedroom doors out onto the balcony and lock on the brightly shining moon. Where did the weekend go? To Venus? To Mars? *"Damn,"* I say out loud, *"That rocket sure flies fast."* The weekend was here and gone at the flip of a switch – now so far away. Then it dawns on me. The weekend didn't go to outer space, it only went to the back of the line. It had its courtesy turn, and now it must patiently wait for the weekdays to play. And play. And play. And then play some more. The line is crowded with work days. It is baffling as to why the weekend, which has so much fun and freedom to offer, has been improperly placed at the back of the line, perpetually stuck behind five days of torment. Shouldn't it be the other way around? Shouldn't the weekend be able to jump the line simply because it looks so damn sexy? Shouldn't the work week be forced to calmly wait its short turn behind the long-legged, high-heeled stride of a delicious five-day weekend?

The way it is now, when the weekend finally makes its way down the red velvet ropes and through the front doors, it is already last call. The fun is practically over. The time left is just too short. It is just too difficult to enjoy yourself when you've missed most of the party. Unfortunately for us, the weekend is almost up as soon as it begins. Sure, there are a few fleeting hours of Friday night euphoria, followed by Saturday celebration, but all too soon, Sunday surfaces and begins to whisper the warnings of what is to come. Two days is just not enough time to enjoy life, especially when one of those days is spent counting down the hours to a work week explosion. Tick. Tick. Tick. Only seconds left before I fall asleep and wake up to a Monday morning detonation of nausea and regret. *Stay awake*, I beg myself, *don't give up just yet*. But my eyelids are getting heavy. Tick. Tick. Tick. If I only knew which wire to snip, the red one or the yellow one then maybe, just maybe, I could diffuse this hopeless situation. My body, ice cold, begins to sweat. My mind lets go and my eyes slam shut.

Boom!

"I have never liked working. To me, a job is an invasion of privacy."

- Danny McGoorty, pool hustler

THE QUESTION

If a doctor were to tell me that I was on the immediate verge of going deaf and that I could choose to listen to one more sound before succumbing to ceaseless silence, I would instantly choose to hear my daughter laugh one more time. Baye is turning six today and she's the cutest thing I have ever seen in my life: sandy brown hair, big brown eyes, and a devilish smile that says she knows she stole my heart. Or at least, what was left of it. She is the spitting image of her mother, my wife, who captured most of my heart the very first time I saw her breathtaking face when we were both freshmen in college. It didn't take long for me to find out that she was just as stunning on the inside, and we have been together ever since. Our little family, the three of us, does everything together (except go to work, which is another reason why I hate jobs) and I love every second of it.

I have been looking forward to today's party almost as much as my daughter has; the sounds of Baye and her little friends laughing and splashing around in the pool, the smoky scents of greasy hot dogs and hamburgers cooking on the grill, and the sensational sight of my beautiful wife, Helicia, in a string bikini. *Only a breeze could louse this day up*, I think to myself, knowing that even a practically undetectable hint of wind would provoke Helicia to wrap herself up in a poolside cloak and hood – with only her eyeballs visible – like some kind of devout Muslim hosting a lunch for a visiting ayatollah. While rooting for the searing heat to continue to boil my skin, sans a seagull's fart, so that I won't lose my titillating view, I am quickly reminded that there is one more way that the day can be ruined: the question. It is asked by little Gillian's nosy mother – the first time. Then it is asked by tiny Todd's father. A few minutes later, cute Katie's daddy wants to know, too. Over and over again, various versions of the same irritating question are asked, spoiling a perfect day.

"How is work?" and "How's the job?" or "What are you doing for work these days?" They all want to know. All day long, I am fielding endless questions about work. Today is Sunday. It is my daughter's birthday. The last thing in the world that I want to think about, let alone talk about, is work. The Sunday night shakes will close the weekend show with a command performance soon enough, but there is certainly no need for an opening act now. But the topic – much like the actual responsibility itself – is impossible to escape, (even on a day off) and that is another reason why the overwhelming majority of Americans hate their jobs. Work, in one form or another, is a continual pest.

My brain is having severe difficulty calculating why these people are so interested in the status of my work. I contemplate the fact that we live in a labor-based society dominated by constant work, and therefore would naturally be led to work-related conversations. But I dismiss this theory after recognizing that these conversations aren't really conversations at all. They are investigations. Quick investigations. Case in point:

"Hey, Spencer, how are you doing?"

"Great, Chris, it's been a long time. How have you been?" I ask.

"Real good, thanks. How's work?" he probes, right off the bat.

"Brutal," I say and watch his eyes light up like the Rockefeller Center Christmas tree. "This thing doesn't stop ringing," I continue, pointing to my iPhone. "It keeps me working day and night, don't even have time to hear myself think."

Chris smiles from ear to ear as if he has been told he has an extra 10 years to live, then promptly excuses himself from our little talk because he is completely satisfied just knowing that I am in pain. I could have really boosted his spirits by telling him that I am trying to short circuit my agony by quitting my job – without another one lined up – so I can stay at home and write for a meager living (at best) because that is what I like to do. He would then, idiotically, feel superior to me and have plump gossip about how much of an irresponsible loser I am for selfishly surrendering from the corporate grind while my wife continues to work. But he denies himself this pleasure by leaving too soon.

It has become Mr. Clean-clear that the interrogators are merely verifying that I am working and that I am miserable doing so. Once I meet those criteria, they fold up their notepads and move on. Elaboration as to what I am actually doing at work is met with total disinterest, almost to the point of being blatantly ignored. My examinations are complete once it has been substantiated that my work is causing adequate suffering and that my misery level, at the very least, parallels their own. If I actually come right out and say that I detest my job more than vampires hate sunlight and contemplate suicide every time I lace up my shoes in the morning, then an immediate mental note would be made by my visitors to add me to their holiday card and party invitation list, because merely knowing me makes them feel so much better about their own lives.

The real reason why people ask one another about work is because they are looking for an angle to feel better about their own screwed up existence. If I come home from work and type out a hit list of all the people I plan to mow down at the office and my neighbor comes home from work and merely pops a palm full of painkillers and washes them down with a bottle of Chardonnay, then, in comparison, things aren't so bad over at his house.

My thoughts are interrupted by Scott, Andrew's dad.

"How's work treatin' you?" he asks.

"Not great," I say in a concerned tone. "I got written up last week for slamming my boss's door in his face while he was telling me I need to close more sales."

"Oh my god, really?" he asks while laughing out loud so hard that others begin to stare. "How did it all go down?" he questions. (Note: Scott is finally interested in having a more lengthy conversation about work because my work situation appears to be a complete disaster.)

"No, not really," I say, bursting his bubble. "I'm just joking. Work is all right; don't love it, but you know."

"Oh," Scott says and promptly heads to the chips. No train wreck here. Move right along.

People love a train wreck (just ask network news executives) as long as they are not on the train. It gives them something to be thankful for. As bad as it is to have to stare at a computer database all day and take telephone calls from irate customers who are unhappy with their service, it is much worse to be trapped aboard a fiery locomotive under 200,000 pounds of twisted steel looking at a shin bone poking through your skin. It's sad, but in some sort of perverted sense, one person's torture is another's triumph, simply because less pain is better than more pain – or should I say, someone else's severe pain makes one's own aches more palatable. So, people deceitfully root against each other (until the Olympics come around, then suddenly and strangely, they root for some guy they never heard of who is wearing a ridiculously tight and shiny red, white, and blue spandex body suit that is vacuum-sealed to his balls and ass while competing in a sport they know nothing about) in an effort to feel better about themselves. Perhaps the instinct to cheer against others is human nature, or maybe it's a phenomenon incited by the pressure we feel from society's gold-standard to achieve at any price. I don't know. What I do know, however, is that upward mobility should not come at the cost of downward morality.

Now, I do not tick that way. I do not think that suffering less than someone else is a victory. I believe that good health, true love, and complete happiness is a victory. Anything less, like hating work, is

72

failure. And my failures are too personal to share with the common man. That is why I do not ask or like to be asked about work (and because not one fiber of my entire being has either the slightest interest in ever hearing the details of someone's corporate job or talking about mine, especially when I'm blissfully focusing on my daughter's incredible laugh as she splashes around with her friends on a sun-drenched Florida day, feeling special because it's her birthday). In fact, the moment someone asks me about the status of my job is the exact time I lose all interest in speaking with that person ever again. This is not to say that I don't find lingerie models, fighter pilots, or circus clowns work conversations worthy on a Sunday afternoon. And, I am more than willing to talk to someone about work in a purely social setting if they juggle Samurai swords for a living. Other than that, I ask questions on other subjects, like travel, hobbies, family, sports, recreation, and news because these topics are both far more interesting and revealing about people than how they are performing at work. Example: I would prefer that a dental hygienist talk to me about her recent trip to Niagara Falls instead of boring me with blab about Friday afternoon's routine tooth extraction. Work should not define people. For me, it merely explains the roots of my anguish. And my pain is growing on this beautiful day with each snooping inquiry about work.

"Ready for work tomorrow?" little Amanda's dad asks.

I feel overcome with nausea and need a break. I am on the edge. I jump up in the air, wrap my arms around my legs, and bring my knees to my chest.

"Cannonball!" I yell before splashing into the pool, momentarily drowning out the work questions.

My daughter and all her friends laugh and scream. I do, too, because I love my little girl so much and because I hate the thought of work. I swim up to Baye and a few of her friends climb on my back.

"Happy birthday, baby," I say with a tear in my eye. "I love you."

"I love you too, Daddy," she says.

"He who is master of himself cannot tolerate another boss."

- Chinese Proverb

THE BOSS

The email is short and to the point and the tone is quite chilling. It reads: *Be out front in 5 minutes. We are going for a little ride*.

When the short yellow school bus pulls into my work parking lot, it reminds me just how unpredictable the big boss is. The tinted glass windows are surely hiding the stern face of a very serious man who is most unhappy with my decision not to follow his rules.

I made a big mistake, I say to myself, while watching the handicap ramp hydraulically lower from the front doors and drop to the ground. Stunned, I look up at the enormous bus driver, thinking he hit the wrong button.

"Get in," he says firmly, not acknowledging a mistake.

"I prefer to use the steps," I say while flipping the back of my fingers several times in his direction, as if trying to shoo the ramp back to its upright position.

The bus driver, who doesn't usually drive busses, grips the oversized steering wheel so tightly that I wait for it to crumble into rubble. His massive hands are in perfect proportion to the rest of his strong, muscular 6' 8" body, which, today, is covered in some sort of navy blue transit uniform that seems too small and terribly uncomfortable. His exposed fists appear swollen with anger, so I am quickly reminded that his nickname indeed fits the man.

"Boss don't care 'bout your preferences, now get on and get in," the driver says through crooked, capped teeth.

I consider the fact that Knuckles is having a very bad day, most probably because of me, and decide not to argue with the man. Instead, I step on the ramp, am lifted onto the bus, and opt for a little levity, which is my strong suit.

"I forgot my lunch box back in the office," I say while striding back a few aisles, making my way to the boss.

No laughter.

Now, typically, I am on board with no funny business during business hours, but I realize that in this instance, quiet is not a good sign. I consider the possibility that, for me, this is a one-way bus trip. I decide to get serious and take a seat across the aisle from the man in charge.

The boss has apparently also decided to get serious, but that comes easily for him because as I said earlier, he is a very serious man. He is dressed immaculately, wearing a custom-tailored black Italian suit, imported black dress shoes, a white silk tie, and a matching white fedora with a black band around the brim that is pulled down just above his angry black eyes.

"Do you know why we are in this vehicle and not in my limousine?" the boss asks, tilting his head to the right side as if he wants all of my words to enter through his left ear first.

I can't help myself. Humor has gotten me out of many sticky jams, so I go with what I do best.

"Because we're going to career fair day at the library," I answer whimsically.

"We have a comedian here with us today, Knuckles," the boss says uncharacteristically loudly, not bothering to look in my direction.

"Seems like we do, Boss," Knuckles agrees.

"That's two jokes now, which is two more than I wanted to hear out of you today," the boss explains in his more typical soft, raspy voice. "I think you should just listen for a while if that's okay with you, funny man," he continues.

I nod my head in agreement, realizing I have worn out my welcome. The bus begins to move.

"To answer my own question, we are on this short bus for the same reason you entered this here short bus on the handicap ramp. This here vehicle is designed for people who are slow, for people who are physically or intellectually deficient," the boss explains, now looking directly into my petrified blue eyes. He continues, "Since you are apparently challenged, you need to be properly cared for, no matter how badly it inconveniences the rest of us. Isn't that right, Knuckles?"

"If you say so, Boss," Knuckles responds, while straightening his ferocious fist into a flat hand to offer the boss a salute.

"That's one loyal guy, follows instructions exactly as told. He is going places in our little organization," the boss says, removing his hat and gently placing it beside him on the bus's green rubber bench seat.

My mind is scrambling to think of something to say, some sort of an apology or promise that will reassure the boss that I am done doing things my way and that I am willing to follow all of his orders. His words beat mine to the punch.

"I had this little situation, a problem I wanted you to take care of for me yesterday, but you didn't pick up the phone. It's not the first time. You know the rules. When you don't follow the rules, you make me look bad, and that's not good for business. No way, no how," the boss says. He stops to wipe his forehead with a blood red handkerchief before he continues. "Now, everything turned out, for all but one guy of course. I got Frankie to eliminate the problem, but you goin' all deaf on me wasn't the plan, and I'm a man who likes to stick to his plans."

"I'm sorry, it was my bad," I plead before being hastily interrupted.

The bus is beeping because it is going in reverse, backing up to the bank of a very dirty and deep river. The bus jerks to a stop and Knuckles begins walking toward us. I don't notice the giant cement cinder blocks and rope in his hands because the boss grabs my pale, clammy face by my clean-shaven chin and spins me around to face him.

"Mistakes, I can live with. I don't like them, but I can live with them – sometimes, at least. Bad habits are another story. Those, I cannot live with. Cowboys have bad habits. They like to do things their own way. You're like a funny sort of cowboy. Maybe you can find a nice little seahorse to ride down there," the boss says, nodding toward the water.

I watch the boss get up from his seat, walk down the aisle and steps, get off the bus and into the open door of a parked black stretch limousine. The limo starts up and drives off seconds later.

"No more jokes, Cowboy," Knuckles says with a mock pout while flashing the pistol that is tucked into his pants and simultaneously stuffing his clip-on tie into my mouth. I can't help but think that one day, Knuckles will end up swimming with the fishies, too. Not just because he – at this point – deserves it, but mostly just because bosses have no allegiance to their employees and are quick to cut ties (or more likely a throat in Knuckles' case) when business is bad.

Knuckles' eventual fate is not much consolation. I think about how stupid I am to have refused to listen to a guy who speaks in a smoky voice and talks about "little situations" and "eliminating problems" and hangs out with guys who have nicknames like "Knuckles" and carry semi-automatic weapons in their waistbands. This time – for this boss, a man capable of killing me at any moment for the slightest reason – I should have followed orders. He is the one boss I should have listened to. When the consequence of failing to do so is an involuntary swim in a polluted river with the equivalent of two refrigerators tied to your feet, then being bossed around seems like a delightfully viable alternative. Mafia bosses should be taken seriously. The other ones, you know, the corporate types, well, they can all go jump in a lake – or a deep and dirty river, for that matter.

I don't like bosses because I don't like being bossed around. I am no masochist. So, the concept of a boss is offensive to me. The term insinuates an inequality between people in a common environment where one person is better and has more power than another. Bosses instruct subordinates. Subordinates take orders from and report to bosses. The boss-subordinate concept is the foundation of a diseased system that plagues the American work culture in epidemic proportions and as a result, millions of Americans are sickened at the thought of their jobs. The fact that so many corporate bosses are actually incompetent idiots that have virtually no substantive insight to offer their so-called subordinates is just an ironic footnote to the fact that bosses shouldn't even exist at all. Grown human beings should not have to take orders from other grown human beings. My boss could tell me to go to an ice cream parlor and treat myself to a triple scoop cone of my favorite flavors with sprinkles on top and I wouldn't want to do it, even if I hadn't eaten in three days. Not because I prefer a cup to a cone and don't like sprinkles, but simply because I hate being told what to do by another person. Employees don't need to be managed. Bad skin needs to be managed. A case of the hemorrhoids needs to be managed. Work professionals should be able to manage their own activity, and if their production is insufficient, those employees should be fired by owners who care about and actively run their businesses. Fewer bosses would mean fewer bad attitudes at work and fewer employees hating their jobs.

If American corporations cannot figure out a way to eliminate bosses altogether in the workplace, then they should at least choose them more wisely. An adult who gets up in the morning, puts his or her clothes on, kisses the family goodbye, and drives into the office should not be in charge of another adult who also got up, dressed, and drove in to work that morning. If, however, the boss got up and put on a full-body leotard and a cape around his or her neck and flew unassisted above the traffic en route to the office, then that extraordinary individual is definitely boss material. If the boss carries a pistol in his pants and speaks like he has cotton between his cheeks and gums, then he may not be boss material, but it wouldn't be wise to tell him so – or ignore his orders. That's where I have gone wrong.

Lucky for me that loyal 'ol Knuckles is not much of a Boy Scout. His knots came undone, so I'm alive to tell the tale. But Knuckles wasn't so fortunate. He disappointed the boss, and we all know how that goes. No, he didn't get written up, demoted, or fired. Those reprimands are threats to corporate employees who are afraid to lose their jobs. Knuckles, however, was in a different line of work with the one kind of boss that should always be listened to.

"Maybe he can swim better than he ties knots," I tell the boss while taking off my silly little transit hat and clip-on tie, stepping into his limo.

"You're a funny guy," the boss says. "Every family needs a funny guy. You're goin' places."

WORK SUCKS!

"Most people work just hard enough not to get fired and get paid just enough money not to quit."

- George Carlin

THE PINK SLIP

The box inside of Kenny's cube is really big, but far too small. It is impossible to fit a lifetime of work scraps, personal belongings, awards, and memories into one cardboard carton. After all, he's just Kenny, not Harry Houdini. And he is just fine with that. He doesn't need magic. Or sizzle. Or applause. The only thing Kenny has ever needed is a pack of Camel cigarettes, a cup of black coffee, and a work station to sit at. *Well, at least they can't take away his smokes or his cup of Joe*, I think to myself while wincing as I watch the poor guy quickly clear out a space he spent 20 years filling up. Just yesterday, during another of our pointless sales meetings, management outwardly acknowledged his dedication to the company and complimented his teamwork for covering the workload of a vacationing colleague for all of last week. But that was yesterday, and now it's today. This morning, he's been told he has 15 minutes to pack up his stuff and leave, which, by the way, is 14 minutes and 58 seconds more than I would need to vanish. My cube, you see, is the same empty cell I inherited on the first day of my sentence. There are no framed degrees, mounted plaques, or family photos push-pinned to my fabric walls because when I decide that it's once again time to move on, I want my getaway to be quick, much quicker than Kenny's. But as bad a day as Kenny is having, it doesn't compare to the terrible treatment Butch received on his last day.

"The Butcher," unlike Kenny, wasn't even allowed back to his desk to retrieve his belongings when he was let go. After five years of service, he was promptly escorted out the back door, like some kind of criminal, with the assurance that his stuff would be returned to him compliments of the fine men and women of the U.S. Postal Service. Now, as rotten as that all seems, it actually turned out even worse for Butch. You see, Butch made it out, but his box never did. His stuff only made it to the supply room floor. In a ruthless sort of way that is kind of funny – unless you're Butch, of course. I mean, why would it be easier to get rid of a person than it would be to get rid of his box? Butch pounded the pavement selling the company's paper shredding services for half a decade, and they shipped him out in practically half a minute. Yet, they can't manage to ship his box, which is absurd considering that bulk mail is sent out like clockwork at 2:30 every afternoon. Even more obscene is that a company that touts confidentiality as a cornerstone of its brand didn't even make the effort to secure the personal belongings of a guy who spent half a decade pitching prospects on the importance of protecting customer privacy and his company's ability to do just that for them.

I slide my tongue across my teeth – trying to get the foul taste out of my mouth – knowing when my day to dart comes that I will leave with the expedience of Butch, but out of the front door like Kenny, who, through deranged, comparative logic got the more merciful deal, that is, if sipping poison from a well-blended piña colada is a better way to die than being decapitated by the falling blade of a medieval guillotine.

While witnessing the savagery of the company's latest termination in total belief, I can't help but whisper that famous quote uttered by a betrayed Julius Caesar as he lie dying from the bloody fists of his own nephew and some of his friends in the Roman Senate.

"Et tu, Brutus?" I mouth softly, while thinking this is one cold-hearted way to treat family. At least the Romans had good reason. But Kenny is no tyrant. He is a father, a husband, and a dedicated company man who actually likes his job and considers his cubicle his second home. And it is because of those two facts that I am totally convinced that Kenny has a few screws loose, probably from banging his head so many times while relentlessly working to satisfy the unattainable company goals imposed upon all of us rats running around this dizzying maze to nowhere. The guy doesn't even use up all of his vacation time, saying he doesn't want to get behind and that skipping work makes him feel guilty. He must have more than a few screws loose. He is completely unhinged, bordering on certifiable. He barely ever misses a day. In fact, he gets me sick at least once a year by coming into the office with a runny nose and hacking cough, insisting on doing his business as usual.

While trying not to stare at his horror show, I remember back to the time when he dressed as Santa Claus at the company Christmas breakfast for kids; nose as red as Rudolph, sneezing like one of Disney's Seven Dwarfs. He didn't have it in him to let the children down (although he probably got at least a dozen of them sick.)

Kenny is not sneezing and coughing now, but he has been delivered a sickeningly deadly blow. I watch him take a drink from a coffee mug that informs the public that he is the "World's #1 Dad" and I can bear to see no more. I sit back with my face in my hands, hiding my eyes not wanting to see jolly old Saint Nick sadly fading away without his trademark smile or his hearty Ho Ho Ho's. I want to approach him, to soothe him, to make him feel just a little bit better.

But how do you tell Santa Claus that his Christmas is over?

"If you don't like your job you don't strike. You just go in every day and do it really half-assed. That's the American way."

- Homer Simpson

WORK ARREST

I'm all alone in my office parking lot but can feel the wide eyes of the law upon my back. My eyes, on the other hand, can't see a thing. I am squinting due to a wild wind that is whipping through the late afternoon sky, escorting dirt from several plots of grassless ground into my face. The dead grass reminds me that this facility is not run by nurturing types.

If they can't even keep the grass alive, then it's no wonder they suck at nurturing their people, I think to myself as I prepare my early escape. Then it occurs to me. I am being too harsh on management. The bosses didn't kill the lawn. No, the lawn more likely killed itself, choosing to commit mass suicide one blade at a time by refusing to drink rather than be rooted in this ground, at this place, at all times. At least the employees get to go home at night. I commend the lawn for its kamikaze decision, understanding that not being able to ever leave here is too big a burden for any organism to bear.

I retreat and take cover behind the dusty brick walls of the main complex, hugging it tightly at the urging of wrathful rainclouds just now throwing a tearful tantrum. It is apparent to me that the crying clouds don't like being near this office building either. And I don't blame them.

I choke back tears every weekday morning when I pull onto these grounds, so I take comfort that the forces of nature see it as I do.

It is time to make a run for it. I take off into the rain to the sound of booming thunder, like an Olympic sprinter leaving the starting blocks at the pop of a pistol, because I cannot bear to stay any longer despite the length of my full-day sentence. An alarm buzzes, reminding me that I cannot get away. I reach down to my waist with a quick hand like some Wild West gunslinger timing the tick of high noon. I manage to silence the humming hunk of metal clipped to my hip, but still, I am hopelessly overmatched.

It's impossible to win a showdown when the weapons that are slung over my shoulder and hanging on my belt are provided by the enemy and are filled with their ammunition. The company's weapons of choice are the iPad and the iPhone and they can take a human life as sure as the guns of a Dodge City gangster, by firing a barrage of work at employees big enough to pierce their hearts in an instant. The firepower of this portable hardware is awesome, capable of catching employees in a spray of phone calls, conference calls, voicemails, emails, text messages, meeting invites, and countless other hindrances. Worse yet, it is impossible to run from their range, leaving employees with no way to completely detach themselves from their work, no matter if they are running to the nearest bathroom or crapping their pants while running with the bulls in Pamplona.

All of this work combined with the threat of being summoned at any time for any work reason can turn a man bitter and cause him to purposely perform below his potential. I, like so many workers around here and in this country, have become a slacker out of spite. I set my phone to vibrate mode to stop the relentless ringing from constant phone calls and reminders, but as a result, I can't help but feel like a rebellious Cuckoo's Nest patient being shocked into subservience. But Nurse Ratched will need to up the amps on my treatment to get me to believe that the company issues and pays for employee's cell phones out of the kindness of its heart. No, this haunting handout – as is the case with the laptop and iPad – is a way of commanding employees to be accessible at all times. The organization saves employees from paying a $50 phone bill each month, but the price of this gesture to workers is actually astronomical as they are forced to sacrifice their privacy, freedom, and personal time as part of this tricky trade-off.

Fed up at all of this, I hop into my Mustang and quickly ride her through the open front gates. I'm away, but haven't gotten away. I leave but I cannot escape. Technology will not allow me to ride off into the sunset undetected and unbothered. But undeterred, I leave town early, breaking company law and, as a result, I will be wanted for this crime by way of mob justice. And they will get their man. My trail is scorching hot because my suffocating cell phone is also loaded with Global Positioning Satellite (GPS) software that enables management to monitor my whereabouts on a computer at all times, like I am some sort of recently reformed criminal wearing an ankle bracelet under house arrest. Only I am not a convict, as I am no outlaw. I am just a salesman. And I am not under house arrest. I, like all people who are committed to a life a labor they don't love, am under work arrest.

The inordinate pressure of a somehow deemed morally legal surveillance perversion invariably acts as a dangerous catalyst that starts me thinking philosophically. This is treacherous, but here goes. I am not a criminal. I have committed no crime. Oh, an occasional lustful momentary yearning or a few too many Coronas, of course, but other than that, nothing: nada, zero, zip! So, what's with the punishment? Somehow something or someone has acquired the despicable, loathsome, audacious power to fill the majority of my non-sleeping hours with pain. It would be vile just to steal my freedom, but the gall to replace it with agony is satanic. What did I do? No, what did we human beings, any of us, do to deserve this? Is it being born? Is this "their" planet? Is it breathing? Is it "their" oxygen? We, here, in this penal colony have marched, fought, and died by the millions for our freedom. We wrote the Declaration of Independence to declare our freedom and the Constitution to protect our freedom. What freedom? Did millions die to save a few hours a day a couple of days a week? We have been sentenced to tote that barge and lift that bail yesterday, today, and tomorrow – forever, for God's sake! For who? For what? Hey, whoever or whatever you are, if this is the gift of life, then reach down, kick over my Christmas tree, and take your present back. It's too damn expensive!

The whole darn deal is rotten, but management recently activating GPS surveillance software on sales reps' phones is such a venomous violation and so unforgivable that it has directly led to my refusal to care about my work any longer. In fact, I now merely drive around all day doing errands and moving from one store front parking lot to another, reading five different newspapers and listening to the 31 flavors of SiriusXM instead of cold calling in my territory as I used to. My counter-intelligence strategy now causes the GPS system to deceive management into thinking that I am moving busily around my sales territory, trying to drum up business when all I am actually doing at this point is waiting around to collect my last $5,000 commission check before I quit the company. I wish it hadn't come to this, but the company has made it clear by their actions that they don't respect their sales reps – and I'm not a fan of being disrespected. I will not wear that ball cap.

So today, I am purposely missing a "mandatory" safety meeting, and as if I could possibly forget, my damn calendar alarm goes off on my phone again, reminding me that I should be in the training room and not knocking off for the day. Instead of listening to our brain-dead safety manger discuss the need to refrain from sticking wet plugs into electrical sockets, I decide to head off into my sales territory to fake like I am working. If necessary, in the morning I will tell the Sheriff that her good little deputy skipped the safety meeting to keep an appointment with a prospect who asked me to provide my pricing. Besides, I already know to bend my knees when picking up objects off the floor.

The weather starts to clear the further I get from the office, and it brings a smile to my face knowing that the sun likes it better over here, too. I pull into a shopping center parking lot, crank up some tunes and jam to the sounds of Bob Marley, pumped that I will be driving home in less than one hour. I notice that the lush green grass at the ball field across the street has not just chosen life over death in its pleasant surroundings, but is actually dancing with me in the suddenly gentle breeze. It's a beautiful vibe until my phone vibrates in an attempt to call me to attention. I pick up the phone, not to talk but to power it off and short circuit surveillance and all other disturbances. Sunrise will bring the law down upon me, but this is no time to be bothered. Marley singing "I Shot the Sheriff," is just music to my ears.

"The authority of those who teach is often an obstacle to those who want to learn."

- Cicero

NOT SO BASIC TRAINING

To the left . . . to the left . . . to the left . . . right . . . left.

To the left . . . to the left . . . to the left . . . right . . . left.

My piston-like legs methodically march me into what is the main training barracks – at another new job – for the next 15 days. Central Command. Impressive, but somehow oddly shaped, I think, while doing a quick recon of the area. The room is rectangular and large and is filled with enough artillery to mold a common pedestrian such as myself into a first-class mercenary out in the field. There are two laptops and one desktop computer perched at the points of a very big, impeccably polished black triangular war-room conference table. Wires are running from the back of a modern hands-free telephone system down through little holes on the table's surface and connect to what appears to be an oversized state-of-the-art video conferencing system in front of a long wall. I consider that the room may be bugged. A huge map of the state of Florida with hundreds of colored pushpins in it swallows up one of the smaller two walls. Very strategic in these here parts, I realize. The metal pull hook on a rolled up slide presentation screen dangles threateningly in front of the other small wall with a menacing whiteboard behind it. My strange surroundings are making me unexpectedly anxious and I quickly compute that today would be a terrible time to be asked to give an impromptu presentation. The thought makes me see blue spots. The uncertainty of my first day in conjunction with summertime brings big beads of sweat to my slightly furrowed forehead that my short blond hair cannot cover. While searching for the location and quantity of air conditioning vents in the room, I notice an old bulky television atop a wheeled stand that also carries a DVD player. *They must keep this around to watch old re-runs of Patton*, I tell myself. I take brief comfort in the fantasy that maybe my drill instructor and I will be watching movies today as a way of easing me into their core.

"This is your bunk," she barks breaking the silence. "Please get comfortable," the 40-something-year-old continues while pointing a meticulously manicured index finger at what is now my chair. I marvel at how a woman her age could look so attractive without wearing any face makeup whatsoever.

"Nice tips," I say in a friendly manner, trying to break the ice. "French, right?"

Her South Beach blue eyes tell me her nails are none of my business and command me not to say another word. I am having a difficult time getting comfortable in my narrow, short-backed, wobbly little chair and her unwelcoming attitude isn't making it any easier. Of all the things to skimp on. This chair is a close cousin to the stool. Having been provided this chair for training, I momentarily wonder if they are going to ask me to ride a bike on my sales calls.

They didn't skimp on the training material, that's for sure. Placed directly in front of me are three loose leaf 3-ringed binders, each utterly stuffed with papers that essentially were printed to tell me what to do and how to do it. My body reacts badly to being ordered around, so I am not surprised when I start to feel the sweat drip from under my starched khaki green button-down. Unable to bring myself to flip open the top binder, I instead stare at the image and text on its front cover. A cadet. Lean and mean. Pencil straight and in full fatigues. At attention and ready to serve. *Boot Camp LeJune*, it says. Bad thoughts start to creep into my head. I am no soldier. I am an individual and have always succeeded in business because of my contagious personality and creative approach. I do not fit well into a cookie cutter system that prefers unison to uniqueness. I am beginning to feel uncomfortable, even uncharacteristically unsure of myself as I realize that obtaining success in this rigid environment may be contingent upon me becoming someone I am not.

I look up at the round clock, which is strangely the only thing on the second huge wall, hoping to find a thread of relief. But the clock has no numbers or hands on its face, only words. I feel like I am in the twilight zone. I read the clock. It says *Don't worry about it* and underneath that, it says *Time to Train!* The intimidation tactics are having a draining effect on me, extinguishing my innate enthusiasm and energy that has been a personal trademark my entire life. The atmosphere is thick with an unnecessary intensity that I am unable to match.

"We have a lot to cover today – and all week," she says confidently with perfect posture. "As you can see, we have a very aggressive training program, so we need to get right to it."

When they recruited me they sure didn't explain it like this. I feel like *Private Benjamin*. All I want is a lobster roll and a nap, but at this point I would gladly settle for the mess hall.

"Do you have any questions before we begin?" she says as the bottom of her dirty blonde hair brushes the tops of her shoulders, almost as if cueing me that she doesn't want to hear it.

"Would you mind if I took my suit jacket off?" I ask tentatively, not sure if she will order me to drop and give her twenty push-ups for making such a request. Sergeant Hulka consents, so I rise on shaky legs, remove the top half of my suit, hang it on the back of my seat, and sit down as quickly as possible. Just as quickly, my jacket falls on the floor. The chair is too small to hang a jacket on unless the jacket belonged to that midget from *Fantasy Island* who always tells that spooky, skinny guy that the plane is coming. Hulka looks at me as if I'm retarded, convincing me that they take things much too seriously around here for my taste. My jacket is now pinned completely underneath my chair after rolling over and dragging it while pushing myself in toward the table. I can't help but think it would be nice to roll over Hulka while I'm at it. At this point, it is apparent that we both are having second thoughts about my employment with this superpower of an office products company.

Perhaps as a gift from God, the instructor's cell phone rings. I noiselessly beg so strenuously for her to answer it that I fear my brain might hemorrhage right on the spot. Only the thought of her not answering bothers me more.

She picks up the phone and tells me she will be back in a minute. Paranoid, I can't see any way that she won't tell the person on the other end about the simpleton she has hired. It doesn't give me comfort because that is not who I am, but the few moments I now have to try to adapt to my hostile surroundings and perhaps dry off a little makes it a good trade.

I do my best to regain my composure, convincing myself that my by-the-book instructor will eventually loosen up. Training programs are a nightmare for all new employees, I rationalize, and tell myself that an intense training regimen is to be expected at a $38 billion Fortune 100 consumer products company like this one. They don't plan on deploying the new Business Development Manager for the entire Gulf Coast of Florida without proper preparation. I loosen my tie, unbutton the top of my shirt, and roll up my sleeves, getting ready to work. It looks like I have been there for a full day when she walks back into the room just moments later.

"HR needs to see you right away," my mentor says. "Follow me."

Idle chit chat is clearly not on today's agenda.

I consider the chance that this 5' 4" ball of fire is marching me into the Guinness Book's fastest exit interview and hope that I am eligible to collect unemployment after "working" only 25 minutes for the company. I am not terribly disturbed by this possibility and, in fact, am actually secretly rooting for it.

*

"Smile," the photographer says before pushing the button.

There is absolutely no chance of that happening based on the way I feel, so I just do my best not to look like an escaped mental patient from Somerville Asylum. The brilliant mathematician John Nash, heralded poet Sylvia Plath, and even the soulful singer Ray Charles were all treated at that Massachusetts madhouse. *At least Ray never had to look at an ID badge like this*, I think, while mulling for the first time ever if blindness has its advantages.

The picture is bad, capturing the worried look of a despondent street bum, but the fact that I'm now wearing the badge clipped to my waistline actually bothers me much more. *If I can't even look like myself in a picture, what can I do right at this place*, I internally inquire while walking unattended back to "the barracks." On a good day, people tell me I look like Paul Newman and on most others I get Woody Harrelson, but suddenly today, I look like some guy who woke up under an inner-city bridge.

She isn't here. I am grateful. I once again cannot bring myself to open the dictionary-sized training manuals. My mind is stuck on how much it sucks being forced to wear an identification badge. I have been morphed. Paul Newman is now hopeless street guy. I belong to the company. I am to be a loyal, unquestioning follower, another well-behaved trooper who focuses foremost on doing what he is told by his superior officers. I decide to sit down on my half-stool and feel like some sort of a stage actor giving a monologue. All that is missing is the spotlight. I go with the moment.

"Badges? . . . We don't need no . . . stinkin' badges!" I say out loud, sounding like that Mexican bandit in the 1948 classic film *The Treasure of the Sierra Madre.*

"Everything go all right?" Hulka asks as she enters the room and hangs her blue blazer perfectly on her high-backed chair. She is mocking me, I am sure.

Her tone implies that she is well aware that I am quite capable of somehow messing up a photograph of myself. If she asks to see the picture, I am convinced she will immediately call security and have me escorted off the property.

"I'm official," I say, the words nearly sticking to the sides of my terribly dry mouth.

"We're behind, so we are going to have to move at an accelerated pace for the rest of the day," my instructor explains as she flips open a binder.

My heart sinks. This is bad. I learn best in a relaxed environment, not in a pressure-packed setting. I don't understand why the company believes it needs to create such a crude training atmosphere to teach its methods to new employees. I am so uncomfortable with their hardcore approach that I now feel incapable of digesting anything at all, let alone moving at an advanced pace. This job is huge. It requires me to cover 400 miles of the Florida coastline and sell products to chief financial officers of massive companies that spend a half a million dollars or more a year on office supplies. If they teach me right – with compassion, patience, and encouragement – then I will one day be an elite member of the organization. Expedite things, and I am a causality of war.

I stare at the very first page of my 15-day boot camp training guide. I am now convinced that blindness does have its advantages. I can't believe my eyes. It's a horrifying daily agenda.

"Every day, beginning tomorrow, will follow the exact same pattern and timeline as you see here, no deviations. In general, you will find that we are very particular about our processes and the expectation here is that everyone follow our defined and proven methods to a tee without exception," the Big Toe explains. "Our employees in New York do things the same way as our people in Florida and California and in the Midwest. That strategy minimizes confusion and enables the company to plug in one teammate for another at a moment's notice, if necessary," she continues.

Her tone is incredibly sour, but at this point, it is actually harmless salt in the wound. A bee sting is no big deal to a man who is already bleeding to death, and I am most certainly bleeding out. She continues to talk, but her words ring hollow like the sounds of an echoing seashell. I am in shock. The basic training agenda is paralyzing.

Each morning will be spent taking handwritten tests on the prior night's reading. Lunch hour will entail a "lunch 'n learn" session, where Hulka will review my tests in front of me and go over the answers. Each afternoon, I will be listening to a series of online training lectures called "modules" covering topics ranging from The Model Sales Call to Procurement Processes and Logistics Systems. At the end of each module, an online test will be given to assess my newfound knowledge on the materials. A score of 90% or better must be achieved or I will have to take the module again. Each module takes between 1-2 hours. My final daily requirement is a homework assignment which entails 100 pages of reading a night. She also tells me that there are a few online seminars called "webinars" that I will have to sit in on as well, which are not listed in the manual.

"Medic!"

My badge is the least of my worries. My health is of utmost concern. I have a little blood pressure problem that may not be little for long. I am completely turned off and quite overwhelmed by the stringent demands and inflexible rules in this work environment. My instructor is breaking me down. I feel like Private Pyle in that crazy Kubrick war movie *Full Metal Jacket*. I hope it doesn't end for me like it did for him.

It doesn't end *that* badly. Pyle blows his own brains out while sitting on a toilet. Me, I just leave a high-paying job because I'm really bad at playing soldier. After going through the motions in a sleep-deprived panic for nine days, I decide to leave before being court-martialed for failing to follow instructions. One hundred pages of tutorial reading a night is more than I can handle after spending my days in a foxhole with

Hulka. I am bombarded with orders to follow, but the final straw comes one afternoon after Sgt. Hulka sets me up on my first of what is to be multiple online learning modules. The module and test is to take 105 minutes. The material is so boring and abundant, however, that my mind constantly wanders. The company makes no effort to introduce information in a creative or entertaining format. I have little focus and even less interest. I watch each slide two times, doing my best to absorb the material, making the lesson 3 ½ hours. I then, still, fail the test. I will swallow a fresh glass of Vesuvius lava before sitting through this session again. I am tempted to go AWOL, but decide to take the higher road and proceed to my drill instructor's office.

"How many modules did you get done?" she asks inquisitively, pin thin eyebrows arched.

"Just the one," I answer, knowing that my service is coming to an end.

She looks at me like she wants to send me to the latrine to scrub the commodes.

I ask for permission to speak freely. My superior officer consents. I request a dishonorable discharge.

She answers in one word.

"Dismissed."

WORK SUCKS!

What I wrote . . .

Request for Letter of Recommendation

6/15/18

Kimberly Hulka
Regional Sales Manager
Office Products & More
3612 Paper Trail
Largo, FL 31265

Kimberly,

It has been about a week since Office Products & More and I agreed to part ways. Although our partnership did not work out in the long run, I wanted to let you know that I truly appreciate all of the training and guidance that you provided to me while we were working together.

In my nine days with the company, I came to greatly admire your hard work, leadership skills, commitment to the organization, and vast knowledge of the business world. Hopefully, during my short time with the company, you learned a bit about my finer qualities as well.

It is with this in mind that I am hoping that you would be kind enough to write a letter of recommendation on my behalf. I am grateful for any help you can offer in my current job search. Additionally, if you are too busy to draft the requested letter, I would be happy to draw one up for you that you can just sign and send back, whatever works best for you.

Thanks in advance for all of your help.

Fond Regards,

Spencer Borisoff

What I felt . . .

Request for Letter of Recommendation

Actual Translation

6/15/18

Sgt. Hulka
Basic Training Drill Instructor
Office Products & More
3612 Paper Trail
Boot Camp LeJune, FL 31265

Sgt. Hulka,

It has been about a week since I quit on the spot due to the unreasonable expectations of your insane training program. Because my employment was a complete disaster from the moment I first marched into your building, I thought – for future reference with other trainees – you should know that I would rather spend a week in a waterboarding torture chamber than spend even one more hour in your presence in that oppressive training room.

In my nine days with the company, I came to realize that you need to relax more than any other human being that I have ever encountered at any time at any place. Still, I am hoping that you can overlook my poor performance under such extreme conditions.

It is with this in mind that I am appealing to your covert sense of compassion by asking that you write a letter of recommendation on my behalf. I am desperate for any help you can offer in my never-ending search for a job that doesn't make me want to suck on an exhaust pipe when my feet hit the floor in the morning.

Additionally, if you are finding it difficult to identify any positive qualities that I possess or are just outright offended that I am asking for your help after making you look like a moron for hiring a guy that quit the company after just a few days, I would be happy to draw up a letter that you can just sign and send back, whatever works best for you.

I sincerely wish we never would have met,

Spencer Borisoff

"Doing nothing is very hard to do . . . you never know when you're finished."

- Leslie Nielsen

GUIDANCE COUNSELORS

Sometimes I try to figure out why my career has gone so horribly wrong. Invariably, it brings me back to the beginning . . .

The line to the intercom is three deep, so while waiting my turn for the drive-thru, I have virtually no choice but to stare at the giant posters hanging all over the building's oversized glass windows. The images on each advertisement look mouth-watering. One picture that I can't stop staring at showcases three beautiful girls dressed in tiny blue and white cheerleading uniforms with their arms under flowing long hair around each other's shoulders and their right legs kicked up in the air. The acrobatic snapshot reveals perfectly sunbaked hamstrings that would excite any 17-year-old boy, let alone a high school stud like me. The bottom of the poster reads: *We are cheering for you to come here!* Tempting, indeed.

They do look delicious, I think, while inching my beat-up 1976 Monte Carlo up in line. A few other posters catch my eye as I wait my turn to speak. One features half a dozen cute co-eds playing frisbee on a perfectly manicured lawn outside an enormous lecture hall. They have a message for me as well: *Toss yourself toward our school – you won't be throwing your life away!*

Looks fun and sounds promising, I tell myself as I pull up to the speaker phone.

"I'll be with you in just a minute, sir," the muffled voice on the other end says.

I am on the verge of unnecessarily answering her, but instead, the vastness of the menu board momentarily takes my breath away. There are so many options posted on the board. The headings are numerous: Jr. Colleges, State Universities, Private Colleges, Ivy League, Trade Schools, Religious Institutes, and several others. Tuition prices are also plastered all over the menu. Some costs are broken down by year, and other rates are listed by semester. I am pretty concerned and very confused when the voice returns.

"Hello, welcome to Guidance Counselor Express. May I have your SAT scores please," the distant voice requires.

"Ah . . . um. . . ten forty," I respond, in an inflection reeking of a question rather than an answer.

"Grade point average," the voice boomerangs.

"What?" I ask, not because I didn't hear her clearly but because I am caught off guard by her detached approach.

"I need your grade point average, sir," she echoes.

"Two-point-nine, basically a B," I explain.

"Not quite," the voice mercilessly corrects. "Pull around to the window."

"But wait, I have some questions," I implore.

"Please pull around to the window, sir," the voice emphatically instructs.

I am no dummy. I can take a cue. I pull up to the window and expect our face-to-face consultation to begin shortly.

The window slides open and I see her face. Her features mimic her voice. She has pale, chubby cheeks, cold brown eyes, a pug nose, and a natural frown that somehow stays in place even when she speaks.

"Based on the information you shared with me about yourself, here is a list of 20 schools you should consider applying to," she says while extending her short right arm in the direction of my rolled down window.

Her arm doesn't even make it halfway to my door. My arm will not reach the list, which is dangling from her nubby hand just above the window frame, so I unbuckle my seatbelt to acquire a little extra lean and stretch. I wonder if she is standing on a stack of telephone books behind the counter as I take the sheet she offers.

"Actually, I didn't provide you with very much information about myself at all," I say, hoping to see signs of human emotion from behind her bifocal lenses.

She is blank, statue still. All that is missing on her is pigeon poop.

"Don't you need to know a little more about me before you're able to recommend a college for me to go to?" I ask pointedly.

"Like what?" she says in a miffed tone while hitting the intercom button and telling her next customer that she will be with them shortly.

Her comments sound eerily familiar and I wonder if my troll friend here merely dangles the same list of schools to all who drive through this place.

"I don't know; like my hobbies, my interests, my talents, my personality, my extracurricular activities, my financial situation . . . stuff like that?" I say inquisitively.

The troll breaks out in hysterical laughter so hearty that the foam ball covering her headset microphone blows into my car and onto my lap. Disgusted, I flick the invading cush onto the floor of my car and wait for her to stop cackling. To be truthful, I didn't think she had it in her. The miserable munchkin is now, of all things, laughing at my expense.

"That's not how we do things here," she says, corralling her laughter.

"I make minimum wage and you get minimum advice. Now, have a nice day, sir," she finalizes and slams the window shut.

I am tempted to drive my big boat of a car through the building, but I don't want to end up studying the Bible at some upstate penitentiary. I drive off, pick up the list of schools, and throw it out my car window.

Now I've been known to exaggerate from time to time, largely because embellished stories have a way of both making a point and making readers laugh. Indeed, I must admit that my high school guidance counselor session was not conducted in a fast food setting, but at the same time, I can truthfully say that the conversation and subsequent guidance I received was almost exactly as I've described. The advice given by my guidance counselor as a teenager was underwhelming and deficient, based strictly on grades and test scores as opposed to my true capabilities, ambitions, and interests. My guidance counselor knew virtually nothing about me, not because I am an enigma wrapped in a riddle and almost impossible to figure out, but because he made no effort at all to get to know me or my situation, and had no motivation or desire whatsoever to do so. His recommendations were therefore rendered useless, and as a result the "system" that is supposed to provide "guidance," advice, counseling, and support to young souls in search of their life's calling, instead, flung me virtually naked into the unknown where I was left to figure out weighty decisions like what I wanted to do with the rest of my life in a vacuum all by myself. (If you are wondering, my parents basically didn't want to be bothered – and that is a whole other chapter – but even then, if they did, how many parents have enough "counseling" credentials to meaningfully contribute to this situation, especially when they are told that there is a formal system that provides "guidance" and "counseling" to neophytes like me?)

I can definitively say that I was never assigned a guidance counselor that made any impact on the direction of my life whatsoever. Not in high school or in college. Maybe it was just the luck of the draw. Maybe influential guidance counselors are running rampant throughout our schools – doing more than obtaining a few objective facts about SATs and GPAs – ultimately pointing pupils perfectly toward their destiny. Perhaps, as a young student, I was assigned the few useless ones in an otherwise helpful crop. But my experience and minimal subject polling on this issue reveals that guidance counselor futility is quite common if not the norm.

The concept of a guidance counselor is brilliant. As a student, my idea of planning for the future was figuring out which beer to get for the weekend or whether to drive 300 miles to see the U2 concert next month. As a result, this would be the first time in my life – but not the last, according to others – that I would require professional help. And perhaps my hollow experiences with guidance counselors are why I abhor the advice or instruction of social service professionals to this day. To be truthful, I hate taking even the most benign suggestion from anyone at all. I don't care that my neighbor had a good time with his kids at the bird sanctuary and I care even less that he thinks my daughter will enjoy it. I simply won't take my family there at the recommendation of someone else. I am a victim of guidance counselor abandonment, scarred for life by dim-witted dolts who breached my trust and neglected their responsibility of helping me come to the most important decisions of my entire life.

So, now, I am done listening to the advice of other people. I could move into a haunted house tomorrow and hear a spooky voice emphatically tell me in a husky, angry whisper to "get out" and I wouldn't budge. Even a legitimate apparition threatening imminent death has no credibility with me. That's the effect my guidance counselors had on me. I weave in humor to soften the blow, but make no mistake, this is no laughing matter. Going to the wrong school or into the wrong field of study is career suicide and will almost always translate into a lifetime of occupational misery, or perhaps better stated, a condition of perpetual misery because we are required to work virtually around the clock.

Now, don't get me wrong. There are many decisions that young

111

adults who are still teenagers should be making alone – without adult guidance – as part of an evolving process called growing up. Examples of those decisions could include whether to attend a bad school play or stay out past curfew. However, when it comes to critical decisions that have lasting, life-long consequences – like choosing what you want to do with the rest of your life, selecting your post high school path, and deciding on a college and a major – that will so drastically affect the outcomes of their lives, young adults who are still teenagers need true guidance, not the equivalent of a fast food drive-thru experience. Life-changing choices are much too big a burden to put on our country's youth who cannot possibly understand the gravity or consequences of these types of decisions. Simply put, teenagers should not be pressured into choosing a livelihood at such a young age. Watching cartoons, going through puberty, attending Sweet 16s, getting your braces off, and experiencing your first kiss are not proper prerequisites for determining one's career ambitions. But the government doesn't care about this perplexing predicament that so prevalently plagues our youth. Our country executes a profitable plan that revolves around collecting tax dollars from its citizens as early in life as possible because tax contributions are the number one source of revenue to the country's coffers. So, as a result, our entire economic system is shaped around shoving citizens into the workforce at such a young age, the majority of people still haven't figured out what the heck they want to do with their lives. So, as a reward, the thirsty, hard-working masses are given permission to drink beer. (Now don't be fooled. While this alcohol thing seems to be a generous gesture on behalf of our rules committee, it is actually part of a cunning plan to dull our pain and medicate a mutiny away, while collecting the almighty tax dollar through state and federal gasoline, alcohol, and cigarette taxes.)

Therefore, at the very least, students need career guidance from insightful, caring, responsible professionals, and not from complete strangers who costume themselves as guidance counselors. My guidance counselors were introduced in a blur and knew less about me than my substitute teachers. At least my subs knew that I was a funny kid with a creative mind who had a knack for making other people laugh (and disrupting class). My guidance counselors couldn't even recommend a good book for me to read based on my literary tastes, let alone advise me on my future path.

So, I have reached the conclusion that although guidance counselors do not make much money, they are still grossly overpaid based on a history of failing to provide meaningful guidance to our youths. They are a significant contributing variable to an American work culture that is drastically polluted with workers who hate their jobs.

In my eyes, guidance counselors are to our school systems what public defenders are to our court systems; appointed professionals who are frustrated by limited time and resources and, as a result, inadequately go through the motions while human lives hang in the balance. The consequences of poor representation are dire. Innocent kids are being sentenced to a future of lousy labor largely because most guidance counselors don't spend the time needed to extensively learn about the students they are hired to help. If our school systems continue with the fast food guidance counselor approach to helping kids sort out their futures, our kids' futures are going to be very messy, indeed. So, the least they can do while rushing to dish out their super-sized slop is remember to throw in some extra napkins!

"The taxpayer – that's someone who works for the federal government but doesn't have to take the civil service examination."

- Ronald Reagan

TAXED TO THE MAX

"I can't get no-oh . . . sa-tis-fac-tion. I can't get no-oh . . . sa-tis-fac-tion. But I try . . . and I try . . . and I try . . . and I try . . . I can't get no," I bellow from the driver's seat while tapping my brakes. My highway cruising tapers to a crawl and I can't help but think that Mick sure nailed this 1960s timeless classic.

As the toll booth comes into view my Saturday glee quickly turns to panic as I realize I have neither the exact change nor the SunPass required to proceed unharassed through the plaza. I pat myself down as if a cockroach had crawled under my pant cuff, flailing for change like an epileptic suffering a grand mal seizure. No jingle. My cotton pockets are silent. I claw through my middle console in search of a couple of undercover quarters. Sticky pads, business cards, a basketball needle, an out of fashion pair of Ray-Bans, and every pen I've used over the last three years. Pennies. Hey, that long lost golf ball signed by John Daly.

My excitement is quickly tempered by honking horns and angry voices from the line of still cars behind my SUV. I put on the sunglasses in a lame attempt to hide and wonder if anyone will trade 50 cents for a golf ball signed by a golfer who can hit the ball to the moon while smoking a cigarette and guzzling a 16 oz. beer. I think better of it and hit the call button next to the wiffle basket to inform highway authorities that I am an idiot. They assure me someone will be right with me. *From where?* I ponder as I roll up my tinted window, hoping it will protect me from the storm of fury building behind me.

While waiting for an aide to magically emerge from the surrounding abyss, my panic turns to aggravation as I contemplate how it has all come to this. Why did I use all of my change in the meter when I took my daughter to the playground yesterday? I still had 36 minutes left when I pulled out of the lot. If I had only played that smarter, I wouldn't be in this predicament now. Then it dawns on me. Why in heaven do I have to pay a toll anyway? Our tax dollars already built and maintain this stretch of road.

The horn blasts are growing louder and longer like the line behind me. This toll hold-up is a robbery gone bad for sure. I'm not getting any help from Merlin, so I decide to dwell on this tax thing instead.

Having to work 50 weeks out of a 52-week year, 5 days out of a 7-day week is a tough nut to swallow, but the government taking more than one-third of my paycheck each week is like swallowing a live Maine lobster without rubber bands around its claws. Taxes scissor my insides. I look at taxes as a punishment for being punished. Work around the clock and split the money, a double whammy for the ages, the scam of all scams. Thanks for the air I breathe and for the loaf of bread and water, Massa. Now please go away because I only have my eyeballs left to give and I'm a big fan of vision, as long as I don't have to look at a work badge with my own face on it. The way I see it, if a government official is not in my cubicle scheduling daily sales calls for me to go on, then the government and I should not be financial partners.

I take a quick peek over my right shoulder and don't like what I see. Arms sticking out of windows on a blistering hot day like today is not normal. Several drivers behind me seem to be voluntarily foregoing air-conditioned comfort to obscenely gesture in my direction. At this moment, it bluntly strikes me . . . our tax dollars are assuredly necessary. I would give my favorite kidney – my mother's – for military or state police protection right about now. Although no troops are rushing to my much-needed assistance, I understand that our brave servicemen and women are deployed on more vital security missions largely due to tax contributions from American citizens like me. National security is certainly a worthy cause for my mandatory tax donations. Hospitals (where I may unfortunately be headed soon) and prisons (where my future assailant may be staying for a while) are also justifiable causes in generous receipt of American tax dollars. There are indeed many elements of American society that deserve to be funded by our tax money, like our court system, state universities, and many other worthy programs. After all, taxing citizens is the American way, so if taxing were done in proper proportion, it would certainly be an acceptable solution to establishing our infrastructure and national security.

Now, I'm no mathematician and I'm no statistician. No, I'm a writer, which goes to say that numbers are just not my thing. Still, an instinct somewhere deep inside my largely linguistic body is telling me that our fractions are off and that hundreds of millions of U.S. citizens are possibly being purposely overtaxed, which makes it awfully difficult for lazy guys like me to get ahead and plan early retirements. I, like most Americans, am playing a game of catch-up that isn't very fun, chasing money that has already been earned but has been taken away in excessive amounts. Now look at me; I can't even afford to pay my toll. Losing is not amusing and that is why I believe that being constantly overtaxed is another reason why American workers are commonly *doomed* to hate their jobs.

Taxes come in so many different flavors, but each kind still manages to leave a horrible taste in my mouth. Income taxes are plain vanilla and come from every level of the government. Property taxes are a rocky road. Sales taxes are old chocolate fudge. Payroll taxes are a flavor with too many chips in it. Capital gains taxes are overly cold and nutty. You get the point. Excise taxes, social security taxes, gift taxes, inheritance taxes, poll taxes, utility taxes, value added taxes, wealth taxes, consumption taxes, vehicle registration taxes, environmental affecting taxes, tolls, tariffs, and business taxes which consist of countless additional taxes like corporate income taxes, business license taxes, self-employment taxes, personal property taxes on equipment, vehicle registration taxes on company vehicles, inventory taxes, workers compensation taxes, unemployment insurance taxes, mandatory disability insurance; the list goes on and on.

It's quite amazing I'm not homeless, I think, as I watch a sweet foreign sports car that I cannot afford squeal out of my lane and into another. He cheats on his taxes, I'm sure. *If we don't have a surplus at the end of all this taxation, with more than 320 million people in this nation, then there is a possibility that the administration has been taking financial advice from Bernie Madoff all these years*, I think to myself before dismissing the likelihood. Nah, the people who run this country are smart. They are not poorly executing a great plan, but rather brilliantly executing a very well-thought-out plan that is very lucrative for the government, but quite painful to the people.

Rampant wasteful spending is a political art form that is funded by tax dollars siphoned from the American people. Congressional pet projects known as earmarks often do not aide the American people who are paying for the project, but instead benefit both the member of Congress who directs the money to their district and the big corporations that receive the money to carry out the porky plan. Talk about a pork project; here's one for ya, literally. As part of a $410 billion dollar spending bill that the U.S. House passed for the 2009 fiscal year, $1.7 million was earmarked for pig odor research and manure management in Ames, Iowa. Now get a whiff of that. Back in '09, our confiscated tax dollars were literally being spent on a pig poop program. It is quite possible that the repugnant stench in the area at the time was not coming from the backsides of swine, but was actually coming from the office of Congressman Tom Harkin, who was born and raised in Iowa, served as a US Senator for Iowa from 1985-2015, and had sponsored the spending plan.

Another ridiculous earmark in the spending bill that should have its lights turned out is a $951,000 allocation for energy-efficient street lamps in downtown Detroit. Someone please explain to me how it can be justified to spend the tax dollars of hard-working American citizens on efficiently lighting a city that looks its very best when engulfed in complete darkness.

I'm not surprised that my savings are not adding up. This can be partly attributed to the fact that I am an accomplished spender. It is true that no one I go out to dinner with agrees to split the bill with me, but instead instantly opts for a separate check when probed by our server. Even my wife considers asking for her own separate bill, but I assure her that we won't be splitting our bill down the middle and that she will only have to pay for what she ate. I realize that the government should be informed of our little dining system so it can implement something fair and agreeable along these lines when it comes to taxes. That way, someone like me, who lives in Florida, works in Florida, sleeps in Florida (don't forget, I'm very fond of sleeping, especially during work hours), and is currently stuck in a toll booth on a highway in Florida would not be paying taxes for a $40 million dollar bridge to be built in a remote Alaskan province that only six people cross a year – and in reality will only benefit the construction company that builds it and the Congressman who added it as a minor addendum to a bill dealing with endangered sparrows (and who also happened to receive a hefty contribution from the construction company during campaign season).

The fact that I have a thin financial safety net, however, cannot be explained simply by pointing to my big appetite. *Obviously, being taxed into partial poverty isn't really cutting it for me*, I say to myself, as I slide my jittery fingers in between my car seat and the console, hoping to find some small change. An ATM receipt reveals that I should not be in this position. I was wrong. I do have enough money to pay for this toll now and on the way back, but not much else. I wonder *what if?* What if the government wasn't in such a hurry to collect taxes and gave its youth more time to decide on a career path? Would I be more passionate about my career? Would I be more productive? Would I have more money in my bank account today? Would there be more quarters in my unused ashtray?

This isn't good, I realize, as a peek into my rear view mirror reveals a burly bearded man stepping out of an F-350 with an angry stride and a clenched fist headed my way. *He probably has tattoos*, I convince myself. As he closes the gap on my car, I decide not to stick around. I floor it right through the gate, feeling like a man version of *Thelma and Louise*. I look back and see Burly shaking his head and waving what looks like a couple of quarters in his meaty hand. I shake my head as I see pieces of the toll gate splintered on the ground. I shrug my broad shoulders. No big deal. Just one more bill on its way from Uncle Sam.

WORK SUCKS!

"What the world really needs is more love and less paperwork."

- Pearl Baily

QUOTAS, DATA ENTRY & ACTIVITY REPORTS, OH MY!

I wonder if this is how Mark Twain got started (minus the laptop, of course) on his way to becoming the father of American literature. Certainly not, I deduce, while sitting in my cubicle strategically punching the digits on my keyboard, creating my own version of an American fictional classic. Our tales are decidedly different, no doubt. Most notably, Twain's works are wonderfully woven by words, while my stories are made up of different sorts of curvy characters called numbers. And Twain's books had, and still have, many readers. My material, although in serious demand every Friday by noon, has a readership of only one: my manager. He does not pass my results along to his bosses or up the ladder to anyone, for that matter. I know this because even a cursory glance at my activity report by a competent business professional would expose my exaggerated data as a fairytale; as far-fetched as Jack and his ridiculously tall beanstalk. Any qualified executive who reviews my numbers would immediately come to the conclusion that my weekly recorded tally is complete myth, but, astonishingly, my boss refuses to see it. Now, let me make one thing clear. I am not a fan of fiction. I do not read fiction, and I certainly do not like to write fiction. I, however, have been put into the terribly uncomfortable and unenviable position where I have no choice but to

SPENCER BORISOFF

betray my ethics and lie about my activity levels in order to meet the utterly unattainable daily and weekly activity goals that have been set for me and the rest of the sales team by inept management. It's a no-win situation with bad choices all around for each and every sales representative at this insane uniform services outfit: either fall woefully short of the established goals and get written up for poor performance and then eventually fired, or lie pathologically about our outputs month after month after month while hoping not to wake the bear from its lifelong slumber.

Below is a chart delineating our daily activity quotas.

Daily Activity Goals

1st appointments held	3
Proposal meetings held	2
Appointments set	5
Cold calls	15
Phone touches	20

It is plain to see by anyone who has an intelligence quotient above "profoundly retarded" that the numbers set above are as unrealistic as an Elf on the Shelf playing hide and seek in your home, gathering intelligence for Santa's Naughty or Nice list. An outside sales rep who has five sit-down meetings – all at different locations – each day does not have any time left in the day to do 15 cold calls, make a minimum of 20 phone calls, and set five future appointments that same day. Further, I would argue, that there is not a salesman in the world who has a calendar littered with five scheduled face-to-face prospect meetings each and every day. Those expectations are outright bizarre, teetering on being so deranged that the individual who links the livelihoods of an otherwise well-meaning, hardworking salesforce to that demented standard should be tied and twisted into a straightjacket that automatically detonates if even one buckle loosens. Now, on top of all of that actual activity, this same greed-soaked madman expects that the details of every past, present, and future task, including all meetings, cold calls, phone calls, emails, messages, and proposals be thoroughly documented in the company's CRM, salesforce.com, requiring another 3-4 hours a day of data entry that – due to time constraints – can only be entered in the evening during what should be family and free time. Well, you all know how I feel about my family and free time. I am not about to spend my weeknights entering hours of fake details about fake appointments for fake prospects when I can be on my couch getting my feet rubbed by my wife and daughter while eating a pint of toasted coconut caramel Häagen-Dazs straight from the carton and watching some crappy new release from Netflix instead. No, entering phony information into a database is what weekdays are for, at least around here, at this job, in this alternate universe. The shame of it all is that so much documentation and records management is required that there is no time left for a salesman to actually go sell anything. We spend so much time updating and adding onto our lies in order to meet our impossible activity goals that we barely have a hint of it left to do what we like to do and have been hired to do: sell. And the truth of it all is that none of us has the desire to lie about the work we are doing. We just want a full day's work out in the field to be enough for those who are sitting comfortably back at the laboratory. When it is not, the "demand more-get more" experiment goes horribly wrong and Frankenstein is born.

I finish filling out my fiction and print it before placing it into my manager's inbox on the wall outside his office, all the while wondering how come computers have done such a lousy job of living up to the hype of being able to eliminate paperwork – or any work, for that matter. *Am I the only person under the age of 90 who misses the world of pens and paper and typewriters?* I mull as I grab my laptop off my desk before walking out to my car. I think so, because I haven't ever seen a pink rubber eraser or a no. 2 pencil on any desk in this office or any of the offices I have breezed through in the past few years. It is apparent that computers have not simplified things in this modern age of enhanced technological capacity. No, computers have instead enabled corporate managers to demand constant work from employees nationwide, no matter what time of day. Computers get folded up and brought home, only to be unfolded and rebooted at the start of an evening shift. Emails need to be opened. More reports need to be printed. Notes need to be entered.

Expectations are sky high.

So is my blood pressure.

And that is as much a fact as my activity reports are fiction!

WORK SUCKS!

"Parents are not interested in justice, they're interested in peace and quiet."

- Bill Cosby

(From what has happened within recent media with regards to Bill Cosby's actions, I just wanted to state that I agree with this comment by Mr. Cosby but with nothing else he has done.. Bye-bye, Bill.)

SORRY, FOLKS

If emptying the dishwasher or throwing out the trash were officially sponsored after school team sports, I would have been a sure-fire high school All-American who captained his squad to an undefeated season while winning a prestigious state championship and the renowned Shiny Plate Trophy that comes with it.

If vacuuming the carpets in my home was a highly regarded extracurricular activity sought out by our nation's colleges, then I would have been offered an academic scholarship to the Ivy League university of my choice by the time I was 12 years old.

Unfortunately for me, scholarships and state championships are not presented to students who excel at after school housework. Accolades are few and futures are foggy for those who are tremendous tidiers. My mother first began leaving me little lists of after school chores Scotch taped to the refrigerator when I was just seven years old. It was her warped idea of being actively involved with her children (my older sister, Bia, also got a list of her own, of course.) I'll give Mom the benefit of the doubt and say that maybe she was grooming me to become the housekeeping manager at an interstate roach motel, but I can't be certain. However, I do know one thing: the broom would have been a great learning tool for me if I wanted to grow up to become a wicked witch, which I would have considered if my nose wasn't so damn perfect. The green face, bad teeth, and hideous wardrobe are major drawbacks to the profession, true, but all of that could have been overlooked for outstanding pay and the opportunity to fly the skies on a cozy magic carpet for a living had that been the chosen aeronautical tool of the witch trade instead of the broom. The broomstick unfortunately lacked the desired softness and space needed for me to commit to the career. Straddling a wooden handle for a living while regularly encountering vicious pockets of air turbulence most certainly would have left me with a bad back and a high voice, which is cause for termination by the Wicked Witch Board of Directors, mainly because it is impossible to be formidably wicked with those two symptoms, but also because workers compensation coverage is cost prohibitive on the man-witch, thus explaining the absence of men in the field.

So, in the end, it turned out that the broom was actually no help to me at all. This left me lost and without a sense of direction. I was in need of a yellow-brick road to guide me. What I ran into instead was a brick wall called poor parenting.

While my mom strictly controlled her kids like a master puppeteer working a couple of marionettes, my dad pretty much just cut the strings of fatherhood altogether. Every once in a while, he would preach about the importance of getting good grades or help me write an essay, but other than that, he was completely uninvolved with his children. By the time I entered high school, my father's music career had reached a sour note, so he tended bar in the evenings for the sake of finances. He was not a happy man. This was understandable to some degree, because it was difficult and depressing for a former teen idol and international singing star to become a suburban bartender. His stage act had given way to an act out of the Siberian Circus. He arose at 4:00 p.m. every day like some sort of recently hibernating Russian bear taught to walk on two feet. The brown-haired bearded bear would shower, wrap himself up in giant purple towels, and grunt and groan while readying for his shift; that is, if he hadn't quit yet. One day, I pressed him for a few legible words.

"Dad, is it all right if I cut out some pages of this magazine to work on my collage project for class?" I asked timidly.

"I don't care what you do. You can piss and shit on the floor as long as you clean it up before Hitler comes home," he said, referring to my mother." (Needless to say, my mother and father are long divorced.) "Lower the television," he continued, "and the next time the telephone rings one more time before I'm ready to get up, I'm gonna wrap the chord around your throat."

Lovely. I must admit that I was pleased, at the time, to have been given his unorthodox permission to do my artwork, but still, I recognized that this was not the type of encouragement and support that helps a young man build his confidence en route to figuring out his future. As a result of poor parenting, neither my sister nor I ever had a chance to discover our interests because our mother and father never exposed us to any possibilities or helped us explore the countless options that the world had to offer.

Children do not have the resources or wherewithal to figure out their life's passion by themselves, and putting them in that situation is a lot like dropping an infant into the ocean without floaties or an inner tube and hoping it can swim. In either case, it's murder, plain and clear; the only difference being that one slaying is immediate while the other is long and painful. Kids don't know what is out there for them unless they are exposed to choices. Parents need to help their children develop interests, discover their passions, and locate a direction for future possibilities. Mothers and fathers need to be willing to get involved with their kids by offering to sacrifice their own time to help meet the needs of their children: drive them to lessons, pick them up from games – if not attend them outright, which was a completely foreign concept in our household – and engage in thoughtful and supportive conversation. Parents need to preach the importance of exploration as much as they talk about getting good grades. Kids need to try as much as they can: blow the trumpet, play the piano, join the school play. It's the only way to know if you have a talent and an interest that can be developed into an occupation.

Mothers and fathers cannot treat their children like a nuisance. Children are not an inconvenience, they are a gift. Parents need to get actively involved with their kids, love their children, respect their feelings, and applaud their efforts, even if they fail at first. They cannot be selfish. It is too difficult for a boy to become a man, a girl to become a woman, and a student to become a career professional. But it is even more difficult to choose a career so early in life that will be personally rewarding for the rest of one's life. It is nearly impossible for children to figure out futures that will make them happy if they have to do it all alone, without the loving help of their parents. Let's face it, when push comes to shove, neither a dishwasher nor a vacuum cleaner are going to provide the answers. And a job as a wicked witch is not an easy one to land – especially for a guy.

WORK SUCKS!

"The best way to appreciate your job is to imagine yourself without one."

- Oscar Wilde

CRASH LANDING

My very first job in outside sales circa 1996 . . .

My plane has landed, but I don't know where to go. Baggage claim is a good place to start but, to be honest, I'm in no hurry to get there and collect my belongings. You see, I haven't the faintest idea what to do with them or myself when I retrieve them. I duck into a terminal bathroom and splash some cold water on my fair-skinned face, seeking some sort of clarity. It doesn't come. Hey, maybe my luggage and boxes of books that I checked at the curb in Philadelphia won't come either. At least then I'll know what to do and where to go today. Complaining has always been a forte of mine, so I can handle the lost luggage crew. I'll probably even make out with a whole new wardrobe in the end. Screw the boxes of sample directories that I need for my sales calls, my company can ship me more of those wherever I end up.

I take the escalator down to baggage claim and wait. So far, so good: no boxes, no suitcase. *I must be the only person in the history of commercial aviation that has actually rooted for their own luggage to be lost*, I think to myself. It's a lot easier to be homeless if I don't have to lug a suitcase and three 30-pound boxes around with me from bridge to alley to abandoned warehouse. My head is spinning ten times faster than the baggage belt now. I am in a strange city that is 3,000 miles away from home. I have no car and no place to stay; I don't know a soul in Seattle. And I have very little money in my pocket, because up until this new job, I'd been a weekly newspaper reporter since graduating college, which means I am as destitute as a working professional can possibly be. That's why I decided to become a salesman. A $26,000 annual salary plus commission won out over passion and talent in the end. So, here I am, a sales representative of a Philly-based company at the Seattle-Tacoma International Airport with no place to go and plenty to do. But the bad news is my bags and boxes have arrived. Now what?

I pluck my stuff off the turnbuckle and drag it all to the large floor-to-ceiling pane glass windows that separate inside from out, warmth from February northern Pacific Coast cold. I can't help but notice the slew of travelers executing their carefully formulated plans: some are hopping onto shuttles, others are jumping into cars, and many are hailing cabs. I usually like being myself, but today I wish I was one of them. I decide to formulate my own plan – better late than never, I suppose. I had seven hours to do this on the plane, but this is my first go-around. As a result of that and my desire to talk to the unusually receptive hot blonde sitting next to me, I was unable to get much planning done. She told me I was cute. I told her she only said that because it's true, borrowing that line from my awesome grandfather, the first love of my life. Cute apparently doesn't go far in Seattle (and from looking around, you might think it would) because wherever she is now, it ain't here helping me out of my Pacific predicament.

I'm in this jam because my company does things differently than most. In an effort to curb costs, the company does not pay or reimburse their sales people's expenses – other than airfare. The business model is simple. Sales reps are shipped to different college towns around the country to sell yellow-page advertising for the upcoming school telephone directory that is distributed to dorms on campus at the start of every new school year. The sales reps are responsible for setting up their own lodging, transportation, and food arrangements while they are working. A sales rep usually stays in a college town for two weeks at a time before heading to another and then another, with an occasional stop home in between.

Now, I know what you're thinking. What idiot employee who earns a $26,000 salary would ever agree to cover all of those expenses? And that is a damn good question. Here's the catch. My company allows us – no, encourages us – to give away advertising in exchange for accommodations. They call it barter. Sometimes they call it trade. I call it stressful. Hell, I'm calling the company . . . that's my plan.

I pick up my suitcase and head to a payphone. I have a funny feeling that my boxes of directories can take care of themselves. They're heavy. They're cumbersome. They're a complete pain in the ass. Yeah, they'll be okay right where they are.

I pull out my own personal calling card and dial. Ring. Ring.

"Campus Phone Books, can I help you?" the receptionist says.

"Hey, Stephanie, it's Spencer. Is Mike around?" I ask.

"Sure thing, hold on," she says.

Mike is the co-founder and president of the small company I work for. The corporation publishes 36 campus telephone directories around the country, but Mike always makes himself available to talk with me when I'm at the office, so I figure he may do the same when I'm on the road. He is a good guy with a perpetual rosy attitude.

"Spencer, how was your flight?" he asks cheerily.

"Mike, good, thanks," I answer. "Everything on time, got my stuff, the books and all," I continue.

"Great, great," he responds. "What can I do for you?" he probes.

"Well, umm, I'm just not sure where to go exactly because I don't have a hotel booked or a car or anything, so I wanted to check in," I say unimpressively.

"Hop a cab to the University of Washington, there are a few hotels right there on campus to choose from for tonight and then barter with every hotel and restaurant you can tomorrow to set yourself up. You don't need a rental car at U-Dub, you can just hit all of the campus businesses this time in," he explains.

"All right; it's just that I don't have much money. What if I can't get a trade or barter thing going that fast, what should I do?" I question.

"Setting up the trade won't be a problem, it's easy. The businesses around the campus live and die for the school; they really support our directory," he says optimistically. "Show them how nice this year's directory turned out and they will want to be in next year's. You have the sample directories, right?"

"Three boxes of them," I answer.

"Great, that's your ammunition. That book kicks ass. Offer the hotels a quarter page ad for free in exchange for however many nights that equates to, and you'll be all set up. Do the same with the restaurants. And you have those Pizza Hut certificates I gave you, right?" he asks.

"Yep," I say.

"Perfect. Go get 'em, man," he says. "Let us know what hotel you land at so we can FedEx any additional materials you may need. You're a natural. Talk soon," he says, then hangs up.

I hang up as well and assess the conversation. Mike seems confident that there is nothing to worry about. And rightly so. Mike knows that his business model works and he also knows that he isn't the one who is one night away from being homeless. I have a hundred and thirty bucks in my pocket, which is enough to get me a cab and a hotel stay for the night. If I'm both good and lucky tomorrow, I should have enough money for the cab back to the airport in two weeks.

I head back to my boxes, and as suspected, they are still right where I left them. I sit down on one of them and think that not only did Mike seem confident, but he also seemed cheap. He never answered my question what if; never offered to buck up for me if I was stranded and on the verge of becoming shark chum in the Puget Sound. Business model or no business model, where was his sense of decency? Is this what corporate America is all about: greed, money, and selfishness? I learned a lot about the business world from that phone call that day.

In the end, Mike was right. It was easy to work the barter system. In my nearly two years with the company, I traveled the country and stayed at some of the nation's nicest hotels and apartment complexes. I bartered for rooms that overlooked pools and for some that had balconies hanging above white sands off both the Atlantic and Pacific oceans. I had my own apartments in 3 different cities and I dined at five-star restaurants where servers appeared tableside to refill beverages that had only one sip missing. I drove around in convertible sports cars and luxury vehicles that are usually reserved for rich people, not 26-year-old beggars. One time, while selling advertising space in my alma mater's campus telephone directory – The University of Pittsburgh – I even bartered for once-in-a-lifetime carnal massages that ended happily for both me and my friend Harkins, who swears that this was a trade that even the old Dallas Cowboys coach Jimmy Johnson would be envious of. Johnson, in 1989, traded away stud running back Herschel Walker to the Minnesota Vikings for a platter of players and draft picks that became the foundation of a Dallas Cowboy dynasty. "The Great Trade Robbery", as it has since been dubbed, was a storybook score, as was my legendary rubdown. After all, I was living on the road, was extremely tense, and needed the massage badly, as confirmed by the masseuse herself. The point is that I received these perks while on the job – all for free. But I didn't make much money while working on that job because every time I traded an ad for a business service, I lost out on the commission that would normally come with a sale. Tired of traveling three weeks out of every month and missing my girlfriend who would later become my wife, I left the company after a year and a half as broke as when I started while becoming discouraged and jaded by the blatant disregard that a callous Corporate America has for its employees. And since that day, not one company has come along and changed my mind.

The day I walked onto that airplane with my career as a writer behind me was the day I should have strapped a parachute to my back.

"Mayday! Mayday!" the pilot should have called out. "Prepare for a rough landing."

Then, maybe, I would have known to kick open the emergency exit door and jump to more hospitable confines, a friendlier jungle. Instead, ever since then, I've been held captive in hostile enemy territory - a place called Corporate America!

WORK SUCKS!

"If hard work were such a wonderful thing, surely the rich would have kept it all to themselves."

- Joseph Lane Kirkland

THE NEW WORLD

"That's one small step for us and one large leap for guts." That's what Neil Armstrong could have said when Apollo 11's Eagle landed. His first dusty moon-step was not particularly treacherous. But leaving the warm crackling fire of mother earth and blasting free of gravity and the safety it provided was downright insanely dare-devilish.

Columbus discovering the New World did not take Congressional Medal of Honor-type bravery. But leaving the safe Spanish shore on a fragile, frigate matchbook was, indeed, heroic. Columbus, who couldn't tell China from America, did know one absolute truth: you cannot find a new world unless you leave the old world.

You cannot be freed unless you break the chains that enslave you. That's the universal truth, even if it's an invisible chain imprisoning you to the jail of Corporate America.

The final frontier may very well be the Enterprise's star-trekked exploration of outer spaces new worlds. But the next frontier must be the human quest for freedom on this, the old world. Simply put, to begin anew, we must discard the old. I disagree with the aristocratic ideology of John F. Kennedy. I say, "Ask not what you can do for your country, but what your country can do for you."

Can a government glider drop you a parachuting Playboy playmate holding champagne and caviar while you suck up sunshine on an Acapulco beach? Of course not, but it can change the workday fraction from 5 and 2 to 4 and 3 – that would be a start! It would be the hierarchy acknowledging the will of its people; a people it not only governs but supposedly loves. It would be one small pebble in one big body of water – but there would be ripples. Who can say where the ripples would go and what they would lead to?

Hey – maybe it would be good for all parties involved. Perhaps an extra day off would translate into a more robust Gross Domestic Product due to the additional time our citizens would have on their hands to spend their money on gratuitous goods and services. Maybe our unemployment rates would fall because companies would need to hire more workers to cover the vacated shifts caused by an extra day off for everyone. Conceivably, American corporations could be open for business every day of the week while utilizing a four-day swing shift work rotation that ensures maximum production and profits while enabling companies to pay us more. Possibly, employees would be more focused, energized, and productive because of the better balance in their lives. Maybe the lunacy of lofty income tax can be replaced by, say, a larger sales tax scaled gradually to levy more responsibility on the extravagant purchases of the rich while lightening up on our totally impoverished less fortunate.

Many mighty men and civilizations have fallen. They failed because no system, whether parliamentary, democratic, or a dictatorship, can survive by stealing men's souls and offering only unjust slave labor sentences in return.

We all laugh at the memorable vision of Peter Finch, in the 1977 Academy Award-nominated movie *Network*, throwing open the window and screaming, "I'm mad as hell, and I'm not going to take this anymore!" Was he a rebelutionary? No, he was a fool. His ranting only gave them notice and a target to destroy. Well, they can't target everyone, not if we all say, "no mo' – make it 4 and 3 if you care about me, 'cause I won't take this anymore!"

The question is: *"What can they do to me?"*

The answer is: *"Nothing, because I am willing to lose a job to save my life."*

And my life is no more important than your life. So, don't mark time – mark your ballot. Don't procrastinate – legislate.

Hey, have a nice weekend.

See ya . . . Tuesday!

THE PETITION

It is with great consideration for the quality of life of the American people, for citizens of this great country of the United States of America, that I introduce this petition in an effort to spur legislation reform that will result in a modification to the standard work week in this nation.

It is with tremendous respect for the lives of the hundreds of millions of working men and women of this country that I bring forward this petition to be signed and forwarded to all levels of government from city councils to state senators and representatives to the highest and most powerful offices in this land in an effort to design a work-based system that will provoke and ensure a more equitable work-life balance where work time and personal time are granted in more equal shares, without jeopardizing national or individual financial security, and thus generating a more rewarding and pleasurable existence during our collective lifespan on this earth, in this country.

It is with absolute confidence that the greatest, most brilliant minds of this nation have the ability to create an alternative work schedule that would meet the interest of its people without sacrificing the security or stability of this country that I introduce this petition as a call to action.

This petition has been established to inform our government that it is the will of the great people of this nation to enjoy their lives through a better work-time/free-time balance. The masses have been whispering for change, this petition now gives them the opportunity to shout for it.

It is with all this in mind that I bring forth a petition suggesting that a FOUR-DAY WORK WEEK become the standard work week in this country.

Please sign below:

EPILOGUE

So, in the end . . .

"Work Sucks!"

Sounds like something that should be written on a men's room wall. Well, it is. It's on quite a few. I know because I made the inscriptions myself. I poured my heart out writing it and even carving it in a lot of little toilet stalls all over town. But, except for a few phone numbers and a description of Lola's specific skills, I got nothing in return.

I use the men's room often because I drink my fair share of beer. I do the brew because 10 hours a day, five out of every seven days, I trudge on a perpetual treadmill that is going nowhere.

Recently, I made a decision to leave my safe and snug corporate captivity and expose it for what it is. What it is is insane! I could not, however, find a bathroom big enough, so I wrote this book, which, unlike Lola's phone number, I have shared with you.

When the alarm clock rings, *Work Sucks!* When you're stuck in rush-hour traffic, *Work Sucks!* It stinks to be critiqued by a boss and it smells to be trapped in another moronic meeting. We are all overworked and underpaid — and they nitpick us to death. I despise the system and the hierarchy's greedy goal of making the fat-cats fatter. I cringe at the presumed expendability of my dignity and rape of my soul. I loathe every hour I am there. But the worst part is that it sits there waiting while I'm off like the inevitable last stop on a hell-train I cannot deboard.

It's in every bite of every meal. It turns steak to dog food. It taints my lady's lips and unsweetens her kisses. It is even there in my sleep, waiting in its starting block for the alarm clock to begin another rotten race.

Yes, it stinks. Yes, it smells. Now, move your lips and say it with me:

"Work Sucks!"

AUTHOR'S NOTE

I have written this book to express and share my distaste for our labor-based society. It's finally finished because I've run out of negative adjectives to add further credence to my perspective.

I want you all to know, however, that I feel no anger or rancor toward the people I've worked for or with. My fellow workers were just soldiers following their generals' orders. Even the generals – although sometimes just marginally – were just doing their jobs, feeding their families. If I inadvertently hurt anyone, please know I am sorry that my indignation overflowed.

I have a family that I love dearly. I am responsible to them, but I do not believe that they can survive on steak and lobster paid for by a man's dignity and will to live. I don't feel that the people I love should be subject to the residual overflow rage I have for the system.

Most of all, however, I want to be an example to my daughter of intelligent strength capable of dissenting opinion and having the guts to stand by it.

So, you see, I know that steak served with anger would not be nutritious for her. Even the vegetables, if offered with frustration, would be indigestible.

God, whatever one you follow, has seen fit to do away with slavery. Hopefully, corporate slavery is next on his list.

ABOUT THE AUTHOR

Spencer Borisoff is a former journalist turned grouchy corporate stiff who has resigned from 30 corporate jobs by the time he turned 45 in order to keep a promise he made to himself as a boy: never settle for a job that sucks! Armed with a blistering tongue that is equal parts harsh and humorous, Borisoff tells the taboo truth about our labor-based existence that, until now, workers have only dared to whisper about. It is a truth that he is born to tell. Borisoff is a Philly boy who graduated from the University of Pittsburgh with a bachelor's degree in English Writing and now resides in Clearwater Beach, Florida with his wife, Helicia, and daughter, Baye.

RICHTER
PUBLISHING

www.ingramcontent.com/pod-product-compliance
Lightning Source LLC
Chambersburg PA
CBHW051839090426
42736CB00011B/1877